Saltlav *(Stereocanlon sp.)*

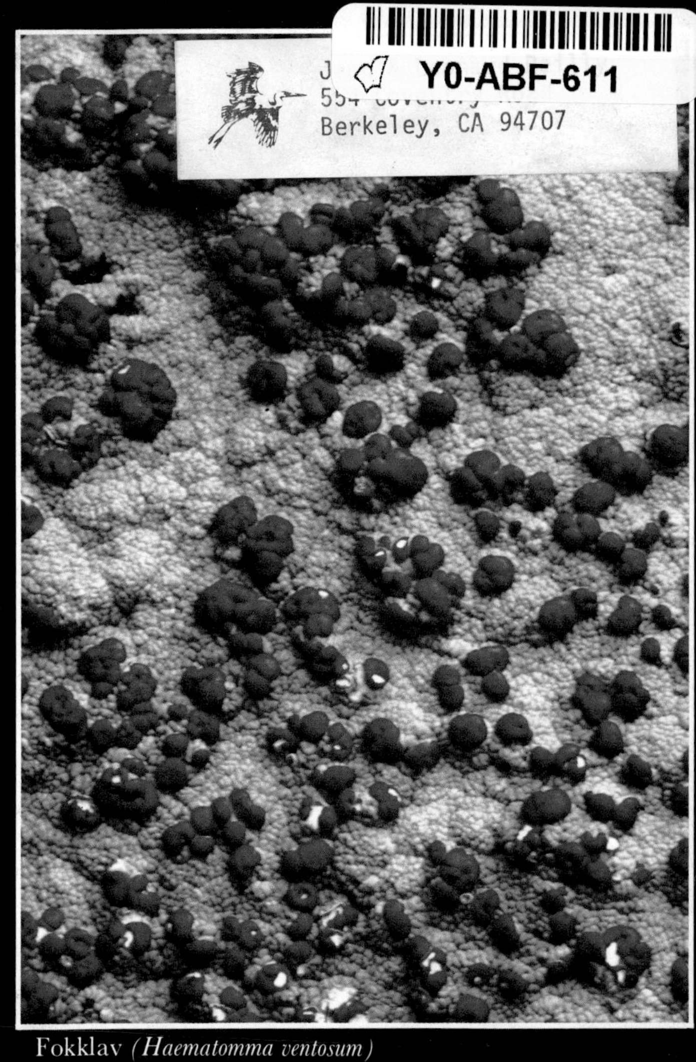

Fokklav *(Haematomma ventosum)*

Gulskinn *(Cetraria nivalis)* Gubbeskjegg *(Alectoria achroleuch)*

Krinslav *(Parmelia centrifuga)*

Page one: A grand old man of Jotunheimen, Anfin Vetti, owner of the farm and tourist lodge Vetti in Utladalen, died in the summer of 1977; he was in his nineties. He had been a symbol of Jotunheimen to three generations of tourists. And like his forebears he had been a huntsman, a farmer among Norway's most rugged mountains, and a friend as well as host to his guests.

Below: Gateway to Jotunheimen – the view across lake Tyin. Uranostind with the glacier Uranosbreen dominates the right half of the picture; rising behind the lower mountains on the left is Hjelledalstind.

Overleaf: Svellnosbreen (the Svellnos glacier) in the Galdhøgpiggen – Visdalen region.

JOTUNHEIMEN

JOTUN HEIMEN

Challenge of a Mountain Wilderness

ARTICLES BY

Vera Henriksen,
Torgeir T. Garmo, Claus Helberg,
Bjørn Halvorsen, Rie Bistrup, Knut A. Nilsen

GENERAL EDITOR

Finn P. Nyquist

OSLO, 1977
NORTH SEA PRESS/GRØNDAHL PRODUCTION

Printed by Grøndahl & Søn Trykkeri A.s, Oslo 1977.
Paper from Saugbrugsforeningen, Halden.
Bound by Norbok A/S, Oslo.

ISBN 82-504-0273-1

Assistant editors: Torgeir T. Garmo, Claus Helberg, Helen Eie Kopperud, Finn P. Nyquist and Øyvind Skagmo.
Cover photo by Johan Brun, showing Illåbandet, north-west of Galdhøpiggen. In the background Smørstabbtindene and Skagastølstindene (Hurrungene).

Articles from the Norwegian edition have been translated by Vera Henriksen.

Photographs by

A-Foto A/S (174, 186, 191, 193, 195, 196)
Andersen, Kjell (95)
Aslaksen, Bjørn (2/3)
Brun, Johan (4, 12 (above), 55, 86, 115, 117, 138, 151, 179, 185, 194, 195, 197
Enersen, Ole Daniel (167)
Etnologisk Institutt (76, 80, 87)
Fjellanger Widerøe A/S (22/23, 30/31, 108, 176/177, 180, 181)
Forsvarsmuseet (69)
Foss, Bjørn (67, 146)
Garmo, Torgeir T. (18/19, 20 (below), 25, 26/27, 32, 33, 34, 48 (above), 51, 62 (below), 84, 85, 128 (above), 199)
Gran, Per (1, 37, 81, 96, 128 (below), 160, 169)
Grøndahl, C. C. (24)
Hart, Kim (17, 142)
Hartwigsen, Yngvar (158, 162)
Hasle, Jon A. (36)
Hegg, Hans Jørgen (20 (below), 21)
Henriksen, Lise (12 (below), 39, 79)
Henriksen, Olav G. (62 (above))
Hovind, Per Egil (74, 75, 149)
Jacobsen, Bjørn S. (40/41, 192)
Kihle, Bjørn (16, 38)
Klaveness, Gunnar (48 (below), 58)
Knudsen, K. (73, 82, 126)
Kongsten, Gro (92, 93, 143, 173)
Lid, Gunnar (40/41, 45, 148)
Lindahl, Axel (6/7, 144)
Lunde, Jon Vegard (15)
Lunn, Ulrik (97, 172)
Lyng, Toralf (77, 154)
Løberg, Morten (63, 135)
Midthun, Nicolai (78)
Mittet Foto A/S (88/89)
Mørup, Sten (150)
NASA/Johnny Skorve (28/29)
Neeb, Fredrik (64)
Nielsen, Odd Sofus (184)
Norsk Folkemuseum (42, 68)
Olsen, Kjell Helle (40/41)
Owesen, Albert W. (43)
Ramberg, Knut (127)
Reese, Bjørn (14, 52)
Repp, Kjell (139, 156, 157)
Rise, Reidar (171)
Rolstad, Bent (153)
Røstad, P. A. (65, 118, 133, 145, 190, 194)
Schipper, H. (10, 35, 102, 110, 123, 182)
Selvig, Marit (125, 147)
Skagmo, Øyvind (134, 184 (below))
Snaterse, H. J. (120/121, 189)
Stabell, Erik (130/131)
Sunde, Helge (101, 124)
Universitetets Oldsaksamling (53, 54, 56, 57, 59, 60)
Vassdokken, Jørgen (47, 70, 71)
Wilse, A. B. (6/7, 61 (above), 106, 114, 119, 136)
Øvrebotten, Øyvind (75).

Left: On the top of Besshø (by lake Gjende) around the year 1880. The photograph is by a Swedish photographer, Axel Lindahl, who has to his credit a number of notable pictures from that period.

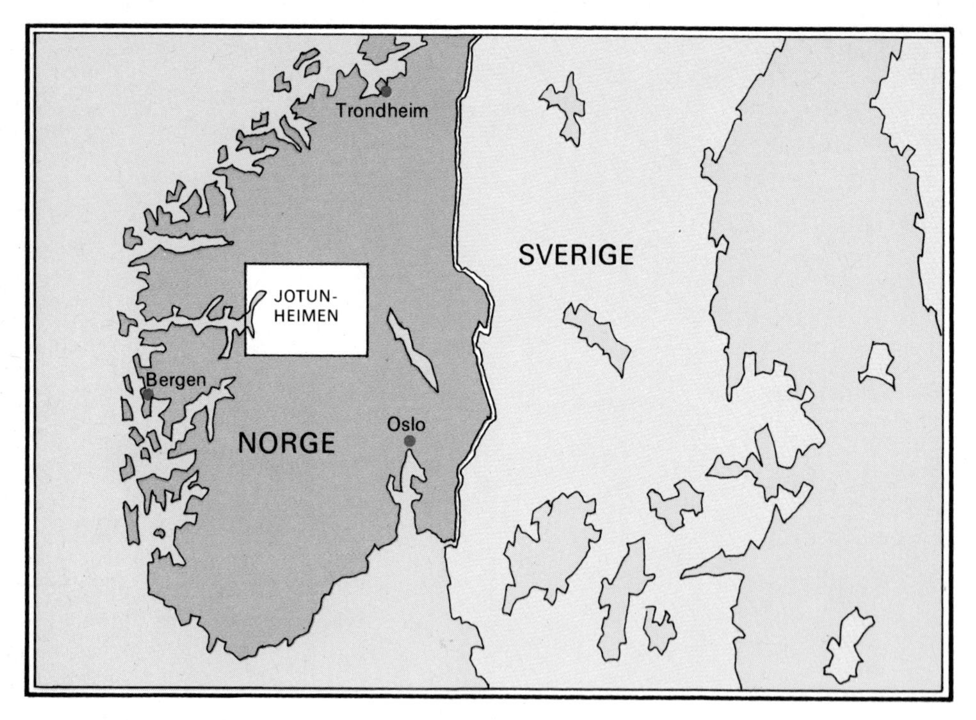

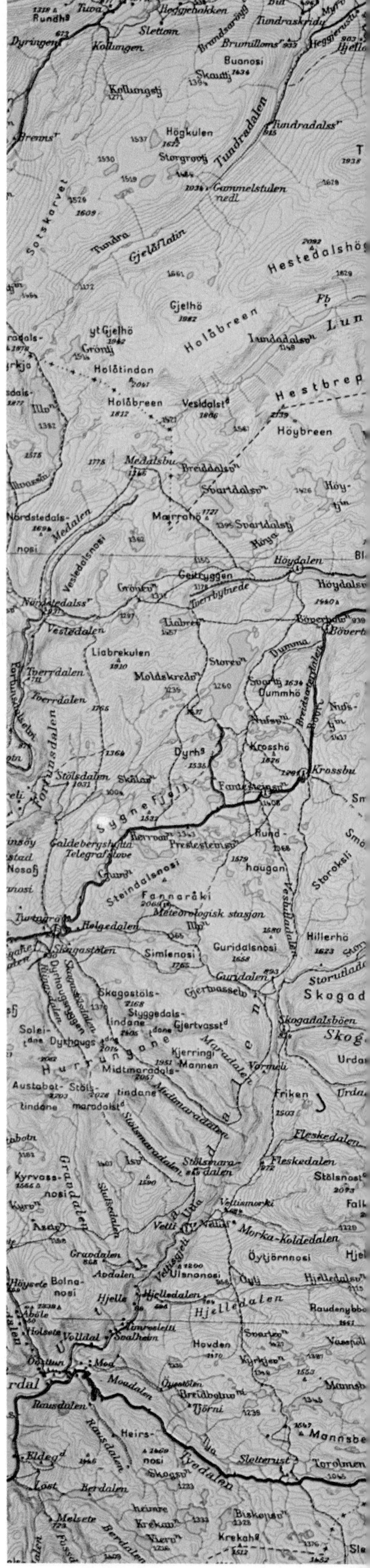

© (Norwegian Geographic Survey).

Editor's Preface

This book is, in its way, a rarity on the international publishing scene. In Norway, as in most countries, a number of books are published to satisfy the tourist's need for information, books which focus on each country's characteristic features and main attractions. However, "Jotunheimen" is not what the term "a tourist book" implies. Originally it was produced for Norwegian readers, a national tribute to our country's grandest mountain area, still unspoiled. Why, then, and English version? Several answers present themselves. One is that foreigners, especially Englishmen, were among the pioneer discoverers of this, "The Northern Playground". And today an increasing number of foreigners enjoy the kinds of tourism that are the only way of getting truly acquainted with Jotunheimen: hiking and cross-country skiing. Yet, we should not have dared the venture of publishing this unique book in English if the author Vera Henriksen (main author also of the Norwegian version) had not taken it upon herself to render the story of Jotunheimen in such a way that it is readily accessible to people everywhere. We are greatly indebted to her. Thanks to her efforts, we believe that "Jotunheimen" will be of prime interest also to people outside of Norway, among them the descendants of Norwegian emigrants to the United States, many of whom have ancestors who set out from the communities of the valleys and by the fjords of the general Jotunheimen area. And, furthermore, "Jotunheimen – Challenge of a Mountain Wilderness" has an international aspect: Jotunheimen is an outstanding piece of unspoiled nature that still *may* be saved from "being developed" – and left undamaged for future generations.

Finn P. Nyquist, Oslo 1977.

The map is a scaled-down copy of "Landgeneralkart over Norge, blad XLIV, Jotunheimen" (General map of Norway, no. XLVI, Jotunheimen). The scale of the original is 1:250000.

Contents

"The river" – this one winds its way through Helgedalen towards Turtagrø.

Roughing It

Knut A. Nilsen

Is the distance from Leirvassbu lodge to the cottage Olavsbu almost twenty miles? According to the time we used, five hours and a half, it ought to be. Or were we in such a pitiful shape? Hardly. We had started our trek through the mountains at Lesja and eventually ended up at Finse, some 130 miles further south as the crow flies – 130 miles of fairly rugged country.

Yet, according to the map it is less than seven miles from Leirvassbu by way of the Høgvaglen pass to Olavsbu. So let me explain: When we skied through Jotunheimen with a dogsled that particular time, it happened to be *the winter of the big snows*. When one has to keep on skiing back and forth two or three times to prepare a track for dogs, swimming in the snow, the miles *do* multiply. We certainly covered twenty miles.

When we set out from Leirvassbu, approximately two feet of snow had fallen during the night. It was one of those days when the whole world looks like a glass of milk, and the light cuts into each eye like a dagger as one crawls up from the lodge's main entrance. Yes, I *did* say up. From the entrance a vertical shaft was the only way out. The snow was level with the second floor. And our dogs, Taika, Varg and Suaq, were nowhere to be seen in the piercing, white light. Not until we whistled a greeting, and three black noses started to move – three huge huskies shook the snow out of their fur and appeared as if by magic. Polar dogs do not run up much of a hotel bill for an overnight stay –.

Well, Einar and I were also equipped to sleep out. But we had granted ourselves one luxurious night between sheets at Leirvassbu. This we had decided two days before, the day we started by hoisting our dogs up Vesle-dalen, a precipice under no circumstance suitable for skiing. The day when Einar ended up hurting his leg and I fell into a stream, and when the night brought a gnawing cold that numbed our feet. – And all this because we were taking a shortcut towards the promised land, Jotunheimen, "Home of the Giants", lying there to the east of us, splendidly reflecting the sunset.

Now, however, rough weather seemed to be closing in.

The snow sighs heavily underfoot as we make tracks; we are wading in it up to our knees across Leirvatnet. Why does absolutely all precipitation have to fall in *this* particular bowl between the mountains? And the wind blows from the east, a nasty draught through a low, wide pass; the lodge is soon lost in whirling snows. Our first mile has taken us half an hour.

No one follows our tracks this day early in the month of March. It is out-of-season for mountain skiing. We are utterly alone, two men and three dogs struggling through some nameless drift of snow.

There seems to be no end to the climb towards Høgvaglen. Fighting our way in short tacks we gain just a few meters by each. All that meets the eye

Left, above: Gale force winds closing in. Time to seek shelter before the blizzard lets loose.
Below: Tenting in the snow by Kyrkja (the name of that characteristic peak means "the church") in Leirdalen.

is white – white – and from the left the wind cakes cheek and nose with ice.

Driving snow makes the visibility steadily worse. As the terrain finally flattens out, I catch glimpses only, of the dog-team less than two hundred feet behind me. But we are past the highest point, treading our way laboriously down the slope on the other side. Two flickering needles, those of compass and altimeter, are our only guarantee of being on the right track. Except for, once in a while, the sheer, black cliffs vaguely discerned through the whiteness to the left of us.

We had planned, that day, to reach the Gjendebu lodge, fifteen miles or so south-east of Leirvassbu. But after two hours of struggle, altimeter and terrain show that we have not even come a third of the way. A resigned tiredness takes over. Have you ever felt that your body is like a short-circuited battery? That your strength leaks out, accomplishing nothing?

Anyhow, we changed our plans and took off to the right towards Olavsbu. With this wind it just had to be less snow up at Raudalsbandet, the pass *that* route would take us through. And we should be glad to reach Olavsbu.

But if Høgvaglen had been bad, Raudalsbandet was even worse. The snow was so deep that we had to kick our skies loose every three steps. We began to feel like fools – for what silly reason were we here in this Jotunheimen, which looked like a milky chowder and was cursed with biting winds?

Then, suddenly, after I had triple-cleared a tack of trail for the dogs for the good Lord knows which time:

The blizzard lets up. We have not even been aware that the wind is

Left: View from Smørstabbreen. The three peaks in the background are in the above-2000 m class: Sagi in the middle, Uranostind to the right and Langskavltind to the left.
Right: Olavsbu. The problem of wet clothing –.

slackening, and now, in a light that grows steadily stronger, we see them glimmering through: outlines of mountains, of precipices, cliffs, an unreal closeness of something that is immense, now the cloud of whirling white is rent completely, all at once they are there, Skardalstind against a shockingly blue sky, Høgvagltind rising and rising above a flimmer of glittering snow.

We just stand there, Einar and I, our mouths stuffed with chocolate and our gaiters with snow. Laughing towards the sky we lift our canteen bottles in a wild, joyful toast to the mountains, a crazy whipped-cream-frosted cake to feast the eye, we are on the verge of tears for the sheer happiness of being alive at this very moment, what difference does it make that we have climbed halfway only, towards the pass?

To be accurate, the difference was one hour and twenty minutes. But our thoughts were on a refreshingly fast downhill run to the cottage on the other side. Our last tack before the pass seemed easy – in the expectation that a fine layer of new snow was covering a solid crust on the western slope. Our dinner of hot stew and pineapple seemed at our fingertips.

All the snow that had not descended near Leirvassbu and on Høgvaglen had collected on that slope towards Olavsbu. We were in snow to halfway up our thighs. Struggling downhill we had to rest time and time again.

Dusk was falling when we finally stumbled into the cottage – of which the northern gable only could be seen above the snow.

We fell asleep with pineapple in our mouths. Outside the snow was laving down. And next day we had a ten-hour trek ahead of us to Tyin.

Left: Mites in the mountains.
Below: Winter morning at Olavsbu.

Measuring the Ice Age

Torgeir T. Garmo

A chilly dawn is breaking as we set out. Mists rise from greenish streams, dimming the gentle light of early morning. Mountains, ablaze with autumn foilage and topped with snow, slowly become wrapped in fog. But gradually, as we climb, sunlight illuminates the haze, engulfing us.

Then the fog disperses.

And after that: lake Tesse, with its waters darkened already, by the approaching winter; the snow on Veodalen's glaciers glittering in the sunlight.

Near the old drovers' hut by Bergenussa snowdrifts block the road. Shouldering our skies we trudge across squishy bogs, ice crunching under our feet and brownish water splashing. To leeward of the steep slopes snow has gathered among the brushwood, while the windswept, bare rocks further up offer a better footing.

Finally we reach the glacier, our goal – see it rising in white splendour towards the azure skies of late autumn. Ice-covered drifts of snow have settled among the rocks. This is the borderland from which all winters descend. And in the frozen silence a question is born: Man, what brings you to this land of death?

Well, to be brutally honest, the cold today is not as bad as all that. And my companions, Hans Christian Olsen, hometown Drammen, and Kjell Repp from Lom, have a job to do on the glacier. They are technicians employed by the Norwegian Water Resources and Electricity Board; two or three times a year they come here to measure the accumulation or ablation of ice and snow.

As we ascend the sloping, snow-covered ice-sheet, a downward draught meets us from the reservoir of cold air generated by the upper part of the glacier.

"Actually," Hans Christian points out, "what we are standing on right now, is not a glacier any more. A ridge cuts it off from the rest of Gråsubreen. And it shows no sign of movement, which a true glacier should.".

But let me introduce Gråsubreen, our glacier:

It covers 2,5 km^2, hugs the north-western slope of Glittertind and, for Norway, is situated exceptionally far to the east. Precipitation on its surface varies between 0,2 and 2,5 m a winter, and Gråsubreen differs from other glaciers in getting most of it on the lower reaches. The snowfall in eastern Jotunheimen is less than half of that further west, therefore the entire glacier is found at a greater altitude than is usually the case, between 1870 m and 2280 m.

"Once upon a time", when the glacier was born, the wind blew snow off the ridges and into the valleys and gulleys – as it still does. As layers of snow have accumulated through the millenia, pressure at the bottom has risen,

Early October in Veodalen, looking towards Gråsubreen and Glittretind. To the left Vesl-Kjølen. Tourists, who at that time have deserted their mountain playground, do not know what they may be missing. The name Veo, used for the river as well as in connection with the valley, supposedly comes from old Norse "viðr" meaning "wood" or "forest" – which would indicate that the timberline in times past ran higher than now.

changing the snow into a plastic substance. And the sheer weight makes the collected mass slide downhill, layer upon layer. Near the surface one may still distinguish, like the annual rings of a tree-trunk, each year's accumulation of snow. But further down it has crystallized into ice, the crystals attaining lengths of up to 30–40 cm. Thus the glacier becomes a kind of rock, at first sedimentary, then, by-and-by, metamorphosing.

"A glacier is like a live creature," the glaciologist W. Werenskiold says; according to his account, the accumulation at the top must equal the ablation at the terminus if the glacier is to remain stable. For while glaciers are snow-covered throughout the winter, in summer much of their snow melts away and sheer ice appears. The border above which, at summer's end, the snows of the previous winter still remain, is called the "firn line". Above this line is found the "accumulation area", where last year's snows are covered and weighted down by those of next winter. And the glacier is like a congealed river, forever moving, forever carrying this surplus towards milder climes where, in due time, it melts off.

"The glaciers of Jotunheimen are shrinking," Hans Christian remarks, as he pauses to prepare his skies for conditions further up. "In 1901 cairns were erected at the snout of approximately thirty glaciers in this area. They now prove that the ice has pulled back hundreds of meters, in one case fully nine hundred."

Measuring the increase or decrease of Gråsubreen. In the distant background the Rondane mountains. Below: With tourists in tow. Indian file on Smørstabbreen.

We stop where a shiny aluminium rod protrudes from the snow. Such rods, used for measuring, are secured in holes drilled into the ice.

"94 cm on pole 11," Kjell declares, measuring the layer of loose snow. Hans Christian duly makes a note of this.

Cutting steps with a vengeance and an ice axe. And, incidentally, demonstrating the three indispensables of rough going on a glacier: rope, ice axe and crampoons.

Imperceptibly the inclination of the sheet of ice is changing as we ascend. Above us it slopes towards center, while it is dome-shaped below.

Not until about 150 years ago did mapmakers grasp this fact; on old maps all glaciers are trough-shaped from top to bottom. And the mistake may be defendable, at least pertaining to "ice caps", glaciers situated on plateaus, their true shape is not obviously apparent.

But in general the Jotunheimen glaciers are not ice caps; most of them belong to the alpine category.

Largest are Smørstabbreen (15 km^2), Vestre Memurubre–Hellstugubreen (12,2 km^2) and Veobreen (11 km^2). However, a great many are small patches only, crouching in the shade of some mighty peak, like Høgskriubreen on Loftet and Bessbreen on Besshø. And glaciers do not all move placidly. Some happen to come to the brink of a precipice, where they keep throwing off large chunks of ice, in the processs forming fantastic labyrinths of crevasses – like in the Hurrungane massif and Hellstugudalen. Famous is the so-called "Fairy tale ice", Svellnosbreen, a frozen cataract falling off sheer cliffs towards Tverrådalen.

The lower part of Hellstugubreen, and Søre Illåbreen, are examples of another variant, the "valley glacier". These are usually fed from ice caps,

Storjuvbreen with Galdhøgpiggen (center). The gap on the left between that peak and Vesl-Galdhøgpiggen is called Porten (the gate). Nautgardstind is seen in the background just to the left of Galdhøpiggen. In the foreground Storgrovhø with snow-filled gillies and windblown ridges.

ablation at the terminus is heavy, and they have a clearly defined dome shape.

Hans Christian pulls at a rod which is tilting sadly: " I guess we shall have to re-anchor this one. The surface layer obviously moves faster that those below."

Measurements at Austre Memurubre indicate that the Jotunheimen glaciers now move at a very slow pace, varying between negligible and 8 m per annum. The forward motion is greatest in the middle, friction causing it to lessen towards the edges. And at the bottom, the rate of progress is 10–90 % of that at the surface. A snowflake descending from the top of Austre Memurubre to the snout, will use approximately a thousand years on the journey, metamorphosing in the process. Which means that the bottom ice now melting off from some of the glaciers, fell as snow during the viking age.

Embedded in this millenium of ice is pollen and other particles giving us information of climatic changes and prevailing vegetation – even of volcanic activity on Iceland and sand-storms in far-off Sahara.

The fact that the layers of a glacier move at different speeds, makes tension build up within the mass of ice, causing crevasses to form. These mainly occur where the glacier becomes steeper or is forced to change its course. However, sometimes smaller fractures appear in the middle of great ice-sheets. And in late summer the streams of water running off a glacier may eat their way into the ice, forming cracks and gulches.

The crevasses rarely cut all the way through a glacier, generally they form systems, some fractures narrowing, others widening, as they descend towards the depths.

And once in a while it is possible to make one's way under the ice, either from the side or through tunnels at the terminus. Under Grotbreen and Heimre Illåbreen there are narrow passages and big caverns where a soft blue light is filtered down through the ice, and the odour of damp clay prevails. I have crouched in there, motionless, listening to the sound of water dripping in that eerie, frozen world – shut off from the stress of everyday life.

That stress again seems far removed as we now ascend Gråsubreen's even sheet of ice.

I startle as I see a dot on the horizon move towards us; it proves to be a man heading for us across patches of snow on shimmering green ice. Kjell has finished his round of rod-checking.

Time for dinner.

A tiny, triangular cabin, held down by guy-wires, sits at the ridge between Gråsubreen and Grotbreen.

"The weather may be rather unpleasant up here," Hans Christian remarks. "Kjell and I once had to stay in this cabin for three days."

"We had quite a time of it," Kjell comments. "The wind smashed the door. We managed to repair it after a fashion, but snow still was being pressed in through a crack. In the morning the floor was covered with a foot of the stuff, and the wind pressure was too great for us to open the door."

"How, then, did you get rid of all that snow?"

"Well –." Hans Christian laughs. "We melted it. And we drank a lot of tea."

But right now, sitting outside, we are leaning against a cabin wall that feels comfortably warm. And the sun makes the snow weep.

"You'd better eat!" Kjell brings another serving of food. "After this we go into the cirque." He smiles at my look of incomprehension. "No gladiators. This cirque is just the half-basin containing the uppermost part of Gråsubreen. We'll try to establish how much water the glacier has lost since last year."

Direct sunlight causes 50–60% of this loss. However, as long as the glacier is covered by white snow, practically all the sun-rays are reflected. Not until the darker and dirty ice surface appears, does the process speed up. Heat and moisture, accounting for another 30%, do the initial job of melting the snow – and winds, bringing warm air into contact with the glacier, are responsible for more melting than rain. Another factor, a minor one, is the heat caused by friction between the ice and the ground. And heat from the earth's interior may melt up to 1 cm a year.

The melting factor makes glacial rivers behave in their own peculiar manner: they swell during hotspells when other rivers dry up, and thus become a boon to withering vegetation. Also, their chilly waters keep algae growth at a minimum; in the case of rivers east of the Jotunheimen watershed

Glittertind at 3 AM, summer solstice of the year 1968.

this has a retarding effect on the increasing pollution of Mjøsa, Norway's largest lake.

But hot summers seem far removed, and autumn now really makes itself felt – we shiver from cold as we stand to the shady side of the cirque watching Hans Christian dig a ditch. A thin sheet of ice can be discerned, separating the new snow from that of last year, and above this ice there is a darker layer.

"Most probably particles of oil and other contamination." Hans Christian gives the spade an angry extra push. "We shall take a sample and find out."

I climb to the head of our glacier.

Glittertind looms above me; I have to bend backwards to see the summit. From my vantage point I can more easily observe how the ice has worn the mountain down, working at it through ages of frost and thaw, receiving and swallowing debris of all shapes and sizes into the bergschrund, the gulch gaping at the glacier's upper edge. And rocks scattered on the ice bear witness to slides caused by this never-ending erosion. The glacier is in no hurry. But countless valleys and cirques are the proofs of its power.

The sun no longer gives comforting warmth. Dark shadows spread quietly on the snowfields, marking the end of a short day. Boulders seem like pebbles in this landscape, as they ride the glacier's back and slowly, infinetely slowly, are being carried towards the valley waiting in the haze below. Contrasted with the blue of the shades is the vivid red of the sunset, reflected by Glittertind's snow. As twilight falls, even the glacier breeze comes to a rest.

The cold is penetrating now. Skiing back to the cabin we make a fast run of it.

Like all cabins belonging to the Water Resources and Electricity Board's Glaciology Section – there are altogether four –, this one is well supplied with food, in case their people should be marooned here. And the Gråsu ridge supposedly is the largest end moraine in Norway, therefore this cabin has been used also as a base for research in quarternary geology.

The huge pile, mainly boulders, extend in the direction of Trollsteinkvølven. Vegetation is scarce; patches of lichen only, cling to the rock surface.

It seems amazing that such a small glacier has gathered all these stones – and the moraine contains rock samples found nowhere else in Jotunheimen. But in the Gråsu ridge, like in most large moraines, ice is found just 3–5 m below the surface; pollen analysis has proved the ice here to be 13000 years old!

For a short while yet, the light of sunset is reflected by hills and peaks. On the eastern horizon mountains of the Rondane massif glow like embers of a dying fire. In the dusk, far below us, Veodalen's icebound rivers are visible – and so is its road, the mark of civilization, brutally cutting through the landscape. Further up the valley I discern the footpath, gently winding its way until it is hidden by snowdrifts.

Dusk of evening at the Gråsu ridge. "On the horizon mountains of the Rondane massif glow like embers of a dying fire".

Tourists from the cities would hardly recognize their summer playground, now subject to that sterner master, autumn.

Inside the cabin the kerosene stove hums cozily, and a tempting odour of boiling meat and broth fills the room.

"Are you kidding?"

"No.". Hans Christian is adamant. "I *did* see the wing of an aeroplane protruding from a glacier. It was during the hot, dry summer of the year 1968. But now the ice has swallowed the whole thing again."

"Some strange objects are to be found underneath glaciers.". Kjell pours himself another bowl of soup. "An eighteenth century pastor at Lom made a kind of map. Among things of note, he included the piece of information that wreckage of a ship, parts of the keel, had been found on Lomseggen, 'evidently Noah's Ark'. But, seriously, in the summer of the year 1975 a longbow fashioned from yew was discovered there. And the body of a man, who had tumbled into a crevasse in a glacier a little north of here, was found years later, practically intact.". Kjell turns the flame of the stove down.

"Some glaciologists maintain that Norway was free of ice during a period following the last ice age," he muses. "And certainly the timberline once was higher up than it now is, trunks of pine-trees have been found in lakes at altitudes of more than 1300 m. But no one knows the exact extent of these glaciers prior to the 1740's, when they advanced so far that they wiped out all traces of glacial activity between that time and the ice age. Since then they have left marks of eight or nine stages of withdrawal. And the pace seems to be accelerating.".

"If this keeps on, I may be out of a job. No more glaciers to measure in Jotunheimen," Hans Christian jokes. "But I could solve the problem by moving a bit further west, where they are putting on weight."

Outside, in the silent night, the moonlight makes the ice look like a luminous, petrified sea.

In ages to come glaciers like this one may be reservoirs of life, providing moisture for scorched earth, and hydroelectric power for faraway and greedy cities.

And yet, in the depths where ice grinds against rock, a process of creation is taking place, new land is beeing formed.

Creation is now – and forever.

Land of the Ice Age. From Vestre Memurubre, looking towards the mountains south of Gjende.

The Making of a Wilderness

Torgeir T. Garmo

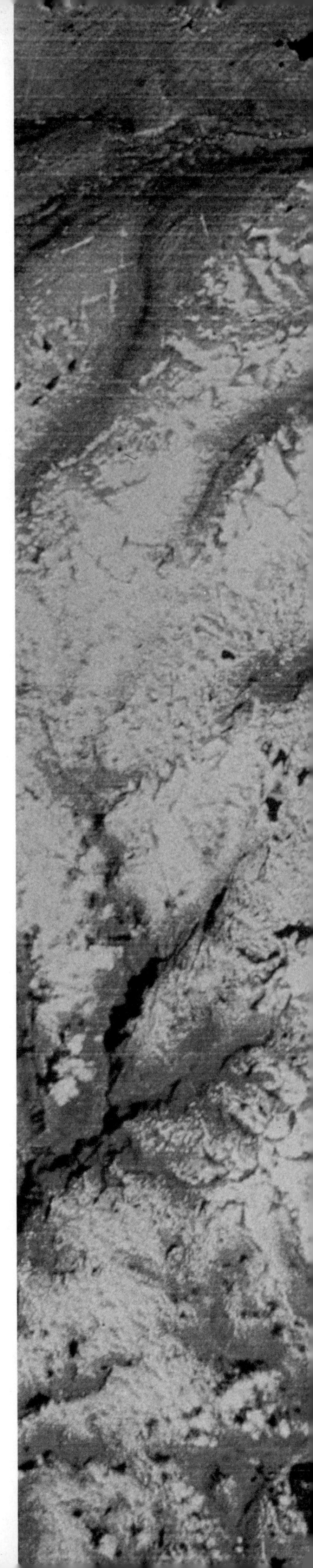

One day in the 1870's a tenant farmer from Vetti, on his way home from Årdal, took a break at Skykkjelneset in Vettisgjelet. Then, suddenly, as he was sitting there, a huge chunk of mountain on the other side of the valley broke loose and came down the steep slope with a roar like a thunderclap, throwing off sparks that brightened the day. On the way it was broken up into innumerable pieces; one of the largest has later been measured to at least a thousand cubic meters. Boulders flew across the canyon, the slide completely changing the landscape and damming a branch of the Utla river; smoke and dust filled the air like a fog.

Not many have, at a safe distance, watched a drama of nature comparable to this. Geological processes in general are infinitely slow; few changes may be observed within the span of a human life.

And in order to get a glimpse of Jotunheimen's geological history, we have to look back several hundred millions of years.

In a tumultuous period during primeval times flakes of the earth's crust were pressed against each other, towering into a tremendous chain of alpine mountains reaching from Scotland via the Scandinavian peninsula to Spitzbergen. During an immense span of time, beginning in the Devonian period and lasting until the middle of the Tertiary (380 million–40 million years ago), these so-called Caledonian mountains were worn down and became a lowland plateau. Then, in another upheaval, the Alps were formed, while this tremendous plane fractured off the western coast of present-day Norway, and was tilted – in Sweden it did, however, remain stable. The highlands of Scandinavia were thus located to the west, with a gentle slope towards the south-east, still a dominant feature of the peninsula's topography.

Since then erosion has run its course anew, eating into the now sloping plateau. Water found its way through cracks and dug into weak zones of rock; crevices became gulches, then V-shaped valleys.

Jotunheimen from altitude 920 km, compare with the map on page 9.
This picture was taken on July 28th 1975 from LANDSAT 2, a satellite mapping the resources of the earth. It is no regular photograph, but was made by help of a scanner instrument with a beam sweeping quickly back and forth across the land as the satellite moved south. The picture, consisting of several thousand scanner lines, was produced by co-ordinating projections of three black-and-white pictures registered simultaneously, two by sunlight and one by infra-red rays. The colours, obviously not the natural ones, appear by means of a special instrument. On this Jotunheimen picture vegetation shows in red, the snow is bluish-white and the glacier silt in rivers and lakes, for instance Gjende, Russvatnet and Vågåvatnet, appears greenish. Picture by NASA. Colour coding and text: Johnny Skorve.

Above Gjende

The ridge in the foreground is Knutshø. The river is Leirungsåe, which runs through Øvre Leirungen and into Gjende. Opposite: Veslefjell, Besseggen and Bessvatn. Nautgardstind and Hestlægerhø in the background. To the right: Øvre and Nedre Sjodalsvatn and Sjodalen towards Randsverk.

A few notes relevant to the text of the article:

In *Besseggen*, the sharp, narrow ridge separating Gjende from Bessvatn, may be discerned one of the Jotunheimen area's several "slips" (result of a movement dislocating part of a rock mass) with fault zones – originating when the "Jotunnappe" settled some 380 million years ago.

Sjodalen is an example of a valley near the edge of the nappe, cutting down to underlying – and, puzzlingly, younger – strata of rock.

Øvre Leirungsdalen is a typical U-valley formed by a glacier – while *Gjende* is a deep trough, carved out when the ice hit upon relatively soft rock, and filled with water as the glacier receded.

Gorges in the mountainside bear witness to the water's power of erosion, and probably date back to late phase of the most recent glaciation, before vegetation had fixed the ground moraines.

Leirungsåe, a glacial stream carrying a heavy load of sand and silt, has deposited part of that burden in Øvre Leirungsvatn through millennia, forming the delta plain in the foreground. Marshland vegetation is slowly invading the minor lakes left in its old riverbeds; brown patches signify iron dioxides secreted in shallow waters.

The talus cones (heaps of rock) marking the lower part of the mountainsides, still are in a stage of development – which means that more rocks keep tumbling down.

The green colour of Gjende and Øvre Leirungen show that their waters contain large quantities of silt and clay – this in contrast to the blue of neighbouring Bessvatn which, receiving its waters mainly by the melting of snow and stable, non-glacial patches of ice, is one of the clearest lakes in Jotunheimen.

Heimre Illåbreen towards Storgrovhø. The glacier's resemblance to metamorphosed rock may be seen by the folds and sharp-edged slips.

The Great Sculptor, Ice

At least four glaciations have occured during the last 2 million years, the Quarternary period in which we still live. For thousands upon thousands of years glaciers have scoured the rock and formed the land. V-valleys were widened into U-valleys, pinnacles reduced to smooth, rounded cliffs. And each glaciation swept the land clean of its previous "overburden", its loose masses of rocks, gravel, sand, silt, soil –.

During inter-glacial periods warmer weather melted the ice, and water again became the main cause of erosion. But a small part of the flora of Norway, and jagged peaks like those of the Hurrungane massif, may indicate that some areas were free of ice – at least during the most recent glaciation. Otherwise all "overburden" has been formed since that glacial epoch, that is during some 10000 years – a split-second of geological history.

Jotunheimen demonstrates this development better than most regions of Norway: From the final period of the last ice age we find end moraines all the way down in Skjolden by Sognefjorden. Eskers by Øvre Sjodalsvatn show to what extent the ice filled the large valleys of the mountain region during one stage of melting; the lake itself was dammed and had its outlet through a gorge near the present road. And the river Sjoa was blocked where it now runs through the canyon Ridderspranget – a broad trench, covered with brushwood, is an old riverbed. Smådalen is another area where the glacier left telltale marks: kames and terraces on the slope up from lake Tesse, showing

Skagastølsbreen, summer 1975. The glacier is advancing, pushing large end moraines ahead.

its stages of withdrawal. And by Randsverk a strange, pitted landscape took shape when ice, buried in the end moraine, slowly melted, leaving characteristic depressions called "kettles". Also: trenches cut into the numerous sandbanks of the Randsverk region prove that the sands were deposited by swift streams of a delta close to the terminus of a glacier.

But in Jotunheimen the ice age still – or again – holds sway. At the glacier's edges one may study the processes that shaped the land. And glacial streams labour untiringly, digging new V-valleys.

A witness to the water's power is the formation of kettleholes; those are found in abundance in the area. Unfortunately a group of them was razed when a new bridge was constructed across Sjoa. However, in that connection a large piece of rock was dislocated and now forms a footbridge crossing the river at a narrow gorge near Riddersspranget – a kettlehole runs through the block, making it possible to crawl from one riverbank to the other. And in Dumdalen, by Bøvertun, a stream goes underground for a few stretches, altogether about 500 m – in the course of millennia the water has worn its way through the limeschist. The river runs in rapids in pitch-darkness; in a pool tiny trout scurry about when frightened by flashlights. Behind this the water disappears into a narrow crevice; the sound of a waterfall is heard, but no speleologist has, as of yet, found a way to reach it.

From Vestre Memurutind. White bands of pegmatites show in the mountainside. Those are rest-magma, last to solidify, and contain rare minerals as well as quartz, feldspar and mica.

Above: Band of pegmatite in Trollsteinveggen, just north of Glittertind. Large crystals of clinozoisite (metal consisting of silicate of calcium and aluminium) set in feldspar.
Below: Polygon field by Juvasshytta.

Bedrock

The lofty peaks of Jotunheimen have proven their durability by merely remaining, when other mountains in the same chain were worn down.

The "Jotun nappe" consists mainly of black- and white-spotted gabbro and grandiorites, and covers the central part of the massif. According to some geologists, these rocks are at least 1100 million years old. However, the confusing part of it is that they sit on top of quartzites and phyllites of a later age. Gravimetric measurements show the Jotun nappe to have a thickness of at least 15 km in the middle, tapering off towards the edges, where in places it measures a mere 100 m.

One theory attempts to solve the riddle of the nappe by maintaining that the Jotun rocks were forced up from great depths when the Caledonian mountains were formed, thus being pushed on top of younger layers. This supposedly happened far below the surface; then, later, the surface layers were worn away. According to another theory the nappe was pushed in from the northeast as a giant flake of the earth's crust, and folded deep down into the Caledonians.

From the nappe protrudes scattered olivine domes, giving to some areas a strange appearance of moonscape. Elsewhere, narrow bands of white pegmatite stripe the grey cliffs; those are rest-magma, the last part of that huge pluton to solidify. Here are concentrated the seldom found elements, for instance uranium in the region north of Glittertind, and rare earth (types of metal) in the Austabott range. Fortunately, they occur in too small quantities ever to be mined.

Underneath and surrounding the Jotun nappe is found, in most places, a belt of quartzite (sparagmite), sometimes with squeezed conglomerate – as can be seen near the outlet of Bygdin. Sparagmite is a white or greyish sandstone deposited approximately 500 million years ago; in a few places the metamorphosis has hardened it so much that Stone Age man could use it for implements. However, in other places the sparagmite is crushed or drusy. Jutingsholet (the Juting cave) in Kvitingskjølen, a druse i.e. a cavity in the rock having its interior studded with crystals, is large enough to room 10 adult men, and old people say it has contained rock crystals a foot long. According to a local legend a dog once wormed its way into one of the narrow passages of Jutingsholet and reappeared in a cave in Smådalen, some 10 km away – by then his fur had been worn off!

The ice has worked its way through the sparagmite, down to the next layer, in that process forming deep valleys. From Sjodalen by way of Tesse, Vårdalen and Bøverdalen a horizon of phyllite and michaschist continues across Sognefjell towards Fortunsdalen. In the upper part of Bøverdalen this micaschist is rich in lime, in Sjodalen it is interlayered with belts of greenstone. And locally the phyllite may be so rich in graphite that one can use it for writing; in Bøverdalen it secretes a black gypsum that, when crushed and mixed with water, may serve as ink.

However, some rocks in Jotunheimen have other, different qualities. A few years ago a lady asked me to examine a stone; she thought she had found gold. A lot of people have been under that illusion, said I. The difference turned out to be that this lady was right – a piece of quartz the size of a fist was covered with glittering specks of the precious metal.

It is common knowledge in the Lom area that gold is to be found among the sands of Bøvra river; according to tradition traces also have been found

Since the most recent glaciation the Memuru river has formed a fan of silt by its outlet into the deep Gjende.

By the path towards Svellnosbreen at an altitude of about 1500 m is found this plucky little pine, said to be the highest growing one in Norway.

Next page: Vettisfossen, mentioned in print for the first time in the year 1822 by the then pastor of Årdal parish, Ulrik Fredrik Bøyesen. He terms it "remarkable because of its absolutely perpendicular fall, as not even a drop of water touches the mountainside". With a fall of 275 m (free fall 260 m) Vettisfossen formerly was Norway's second highest, but recently has gained status of the highest – this because the waters of Mardølafossen, with a free fall of 297 m (Northern Europe's highest) have been diverted for hydroelectric purposes.

in Visdalen. The source is most likely located in one of the white veins of quartzite in the precipices high above Visa or Bøvra. Anybody is free to look for it. But the search is guaranteed to be a breakneck venture.

From Stone to Soil

Moraines left by the ice are an unsorted mixture of rocks, varying in size from boulders to infinitesimal grains of clay.

But the rivers, for instance those from Memurubreen, immediately begin a process of sorting this overburden according to sizes. Large rocks are left in the riverbeds as soon as the stream slows down to a reasonable pace. And numerous gravel beds are found in the lower reaches of the Memuru river. In Gjende clay and silt is laid off, accounting for the green colour of that lake. The colour does, however, become less pronounced as the lake's waters flow from Memurubu towards the outlet by Gjendesheim, depositing quite a bit of ooze on the bottom. And the Sjoa river gradually gets clearer as it makes its way through lakes and is diluted by tributaries.

But some glacial rivers have little or no opportunity of depositing their loads of sand, silt and clay. On a warm summer's day Storbekken in Leirdalen carries 10 tons of such matter an hour. And Leira and Bøvra, green in spring, become grey and soupy during hot summers, and through the centuries their riverbeds keep rising. At the delta where Bøvre empties into Skim, more than 10000 tons of sand and silt is deposited annually.

At high altitudes a different sorting process takes place, the frost and thaw disposing the various grades of soil in their own peculiar manner. In the tundra region, only the uppermost layer ever thaws. If on a slope, that layer in summer keeps drifting slowly downwards on top of the permafrost, while a rough sorting automatically takes place. On moist plateaus the frost arranges the gravel in a pattern of polygons, with the finer grades towards centre; the effect of this may be seen in the vicinity of Juvasshytta.

The Silent Conquest

While the ice was loosening its grip on the mountains, the plants did not tarry long before their invasion began. A rough idea of the order of arrival of various species may be had by taking stock of their hardiness – the hardiest ones, those which in our times are found at the higher altitudes, most likely were the earlier to appear.

According to this rule-of-thumb (and discounting the possibility that some early species may have become extinct, also the theory that certain species may have survived in Jotunheimen during the most recent glacial epoch), the lichens and mosses came first. Some grasses and sedges followed in quick succession. Arriving next were various kinds of willow bushes, the juniper and the dwarf birch. Then came the trees, and their importance is evident by the term "timberline", meaning the border above which trees will not grow. The mountain birch, hardy variant of the common birch, probably led the way, followed by some other types of deciduous trees. At about the same time the pine (Pinus sylvestris) made its appearance. These trees, found west as well as east of Jotunheimen, supposedly made their way across the mountains during one of the spells of warm weather prevailing in the latter part of the Stone Age and the Bronze Age (up to about 500 BC). The climate then changed for the worse, som climatologists think that happened quite abruptly.

And the timberline, which had been at least a couple of hundred meters higher up than it now is, receded. After that, too late to make it across the mountains on its own, a new-comer arrived – which became known as the Norwegian spruce (Picea ábies). And, of course, a number of less noticeable plants established themselves simultanously with these dominant species.

However, when gneissic gabbros decompose, the resulting soil is relatively barren – the same goes for quartzite. Great parts of Jotunheimen therefore have a sparse and fairly undiversified flora. Still, conditions vary.

Thus, on the shores of Bøvertunvatnet (alt. 939 m), where the soil is rich in lime, a lush flora is found, including a couple of species of orchids and, most noticable, the "reindeer rose" (Dryas octopétala) covering whole mountain-sides with its white flowers. Lime-rich soil offers excellent conditions also for the most flamboyant flower of the region, the purple saxifrage. The botanist Knut Fægri writes: "If skiing in spring through a landscape dominated by white snow and greyish-black rocks, one suddenly has come upon a cliff covered with exotic reddish-violet flowers, of a hue not quite matched by any others in our flora, then one has gotten a shock – and at the same time has been enriched by an experience never to be forgotten."

Phyllite also gives fertile soil, and an area especially attractive to botanists is the Såleggen-Smådalen region. Here are found, among many other species, an extremely rare Saxifraga, the S. foliolósa, which unfortunately very seldom blooms, and a local sub-species of mountain poppy (Papaver rádicátum). And the northern shore of Gjende, not having been thoroughly explorded geologically, nevertheless offers an abundant flora. In the vicinity of Gjendebu some 700 different species have been found at altitudes of 1000–1500 m. Furthermore, a special flora, nourished by a soil rich in iron and magnesium, is to be found where olivine domes protrude from the Jotun nappe – here the lovely alpine campion abounds.

But factors other than soil conditions are of importance: the supply of water – som plants prefer bogs, others relatively arid land –; the thickness of the snow cover – some plants thrive where the snow has stayed late in spring, others on windblown ridges where it melts early, but where moisture may be in short supply –.

Left: Snowed in and dwarfed by mighty surroundings. The Norwegian Tourist Association's lodge Skogadalsbøen (Utladalen) in the middle of winter.
Right: Torfinnsbu lodge by Bygdin. This lodge, formerly belonging to the Tourist Association, but now privately owned, is partly built from timber from the very first lodge raised by the Association in Jotunheimen: Tvinnehaugen (Tvindehougen) by Tyin, opened to guests the summer of 1871 (page 143).

1. Purple saxifrage *(Saxifraga oppositifólia)*, early messenger of spring in the mountains. 2. Alpine hawkweed, one of many sub-species of *Hieracium*. 3. Alpine willow *(Salix herbacéa)*, very common in Jotunheimen. Linné termed it "the smallest tree in the world". 4. *Gentiána nivális*, known as "snøsøte" ("snow gentian"). 5. Alpine crowfoot *(Ranúnculus glaciális)* is found at a higher altitude than any other flower in Norway. 6. *Pulsatilla vernális*, "mogop", a relative of the pasque flower. And not only bees, but an ant, may unwittingly assist in the process of fertilizing a flower. 7. Roseroot *(Sédum rósea)* conserves moisture, and for that reason has frequently been planted on sod roofs as a protection against sparks from the chimney. 8. Alpine campion *(Viscária alpina)* prefers soil rich in iron and other metals, and in Jotunheimen is found up to an altiude of 1900 m. 9. *Pfyllódoce coerúlea* is known as "blålyng", «blue heather», even though its flowers are reddish or violet in the beginning.

5
7
8
9

End of a bruin. The result of a successful bear hunt in the Vestre Slidre (Valdres) in the year 1896.

Most important of all is the altitude; this is evident by the fact that mountain areas are divided into altitude zones according to the vegetation.

However, below those zones and still definitely part of Jotunheimen are the forests of evergreen; some of the valleys cutting deep into the mountain region give excellent conditions for these trees. Pine forests are found up to an altitude of 1050 m (in Visdalen).

But the best known pine forest is that of Vettismorki, situated in a wide valley at altitudes between 650 and 800 m, and coming to the brink of the precipice where the magnificent Vettisfossen makes a free dive of 260 m to the floor of Utladalen. In the year 1822 a local pastor mentioned this forest, calling it "one of the most wonderful forests of the diocese ... Here grow, unused and unusable because the logs would be reduced to splinters if floated down Vettisfossen, tall pines of extraordinary girth." Yet a way was found to get the timber out. Wm. Cecil Slingsby recalls from his visit to Vettisfossen in 1874: "Many pine-trees, stripped of their branches, will be seen below the fall, and a close examination of the cliff above will reveal a timber-shoot made of trees projecting twelve or fourteen feet over the cliff. Down this shoot the big trees are precipitated in winter into the awful gulf, a good eight seconds elapsing before they touch the snow below. Many are splintered and broken, but still it pays, and Norsemen are very careless about the disappearance of their forests.". Incidentally, this operation took place late in winter, when a pile of ice, snow and rime had collected under the fall, forming a kind of cushion on which the logs landed.

The Vettismorki forest now stands unmolested, protected by law, except from the smoke spewed out by the aluminium works at Årdal.

The spruce is less suited than the pine to mountain life. A shallow root system reduces its ability to withstand dry-spells and causes it to be rather easily overturned by strong winds. And at high altitudes it has difficulty bringing forth cones; it therefore spreads by shoots. Yet spruce is common to the forested valleys east of the watershed.

But birch woods make their way into the mountain area everywhere, and they climb high – in Utladalen and Smådalen up to 1100 m, in Sikkilsdalen to 1120 m. On the lower reaches these birch forests are mixed with rowan and aspen; specimens of alder and bird cherry are also found. And on the forest floor willows, ferns and various other plants: monk's hood, alpine lettuce, globe flower, angelica, wood cranesbill – grow in such abundance that, if leaving the path, one may find one's progress practically blocked. In the high birch woods vegetation is less profuse. On the dry forest floor cowberry (lingonberry), whortleberry, heather and an assortment of tiny flowers may be found.

And in this so-called "sub-alpine" zone of birch woods the summer farms are usually located, as the mountain grasses offer excellent pastures.

The lower alpine zone, where bushy willows, dwarf birch and juniper reign, reach an altitude of 1300–1400 m. Among these bushes grow crowberry, Scottish menzensia, alpine bearberry, bog whortleberry –. Early in spring blooms the "mogop", cuddly cousin to the pasque flower; soon after that the purple flowers of the "lapprose" appear – a tiny member of the rhododendron family, and one of the plants botanists speculate may have survived the last ice age in Norway. Whortleberry heath marks the upper border of this zone.

Above is the region where grasses, sedges and heather prevail. And on marsh-lands cottongrass and some species of saxifraga grow. But as the altitude increases, mosses and lichens gain in importance. In the eastern part of this high alpine zone lichens may cover whole mountainsides, giving them a dull, grey hue. And except for the lichens, the upper reaches seem barren. Yet the botanist Reidar Jørgensen managed to find 36 different species of vascular

The glutton's main prey is reindeer, mainly sick or weak animals. The picture is not from Jotunheimen.

plants above the altitude of 2000 m – highest grew the alpine crowfoot, found at 2370 m on Galdhøpiggen.

Of Birds and Beasts

Between ice ages, and possibly towards the end of the last one, a shaggy giant made the Jotunheimen region its home: the mammoth. Parts of a mammoth molar have been found at Skårvangen in Vågå, and a tusk near Lesja.

We also know that reindeer and other animals, adjusted to a rough climate, arrived in Jotunheimen as soon as there were plants suitable for them to eat – and that predators followed. As for the fauna of a later age, we shall turn to Mr. Slingsby's account from the 1870's:

"Jotunheimen is rich in animal life. The bear undoubtedly is king, but, though traces of him may be found almost everywhere, he does not often allow himself to be seen. He has a formidable rival in the Glutton, which, unlike the bear, is entirely carnivorous, and many a full-grown, as well as a young, reindeer falls a prey to this ferocious beast. The farmer, as a rule, detests the Glutton, while he often has a sneaking affection for the Bear. The Lynx kills many a kid, and the Fox, which is larger and handsomer than his English brother, whose cunning he shares, roames over the whole land. The Wolf, common enough forty years ago, is now extinct. Reindeer are still seen on the fjeld, but until they were scared away by tourists, large and numerous herds were frequently met with. Red deer occasionally pay northern Jotunheimen a visit, as do Elk the southern portion. The Otter frequents the lakes and rivers. Squirrels disport themselves in the pine-trees, and in the winter time turn grey – the colour well known to ladies who encourage the slaughter of these beautiful creatures by wearing fur cloaks made of Squirrel skins. The Ermine is pretty common – I once saw about a dozen of them in Helgedal in winter. The peripathetic and pugnatious little Lemming appears and disappears in Jotunheimen as it does elsewhere in Norway, and is followed on foot by his enemies the Glutton, the Lynx, and the Fox, and in the air above him by the Snowy Owl, Eagles, various kind of Hawks, and the Raven.

In addition to the birds of prey, many feathered friends greet us in Jotunheimen. Several sorts of Tomtits, as perky as they are here (in England), Larks, Finches, Buntings, Redpolls, Snipe, Waterfowl in great variety, Sandpipers, Wagtails, Warblers, Redwings, Fieldfares. As I am not an autioneer, I will not make anything like a complete list. There must, however, be added the Dipper, or Water-Ouzel, which remains in the north through fair weather and foul, through the heat of summer and the snows of winter. The sight of this beautiful bird is more welcome to me than that of any other which I see in Norway –." I certainly shall not attempt to complete his list. It may, however, be of interest to add a few species and some commentaries.

Among the mammals should be mentioned the marten, native to the region from way back. But martens are rare today; the high prize of their skins has been a disaster to the species. Also deserving of mention is the polar fox, whose trusting curiosity and valuable pelt has cost him even more dearly. Polar foxes had not been observed in Jotunheimen for a good many years, until recently, when a few sightings have been reported.

And Mr. Slingsby has, surprisingly, omitted the typical gamebirds: the "fjellrype" (a ptarmigan), the "lirype" (a grouse), the black grouse and the capercaillie. The first is mainly found in the alpine zone, the second in the sub-alpine "birch belt", the latter two dwell in the forested valleys. These

1. Ptarmigan cock in the mottled coat of early spring. 2. Dotterel plover, a bird that is trusting to the point of silliness. 3. Snow bunting, an unassuming little fellow that thrives where other birds can not make out. 4. Golden plover, better known by its flute-like call than by its looks. 5. Common snipes. In a folk-tale a snipe mother bird begs a hunter not to shoot her chicks, exclaiming that they are the most beautiful of all birds. Later, when he has bagged her whole brood, she bitterly reproaches him, and he, stunned, protests that he has shot the homeliest birds he saw. Hence the expression "snipe mother".

birds have been severely taxed and their numbers greatly reduced. Towards the end of the 1950's huge flocks of ptarmigan could be seen rising when startled, disappearing like white clouds on the horizon. Now one rarely hears a "rype" cock cackle. Admittedly, their numbers always have varied a great deal from one year to another. But they now seem to have reached an all-time low, hopefully not a point of no return.

Then it may be of interest that buzzards are fairly common in the district, as the large rough-leg occasionally is mistaken for an eagle.

A couple of plovers also deserve mention, as they are noticed by most visitors to Jotunheimen. The female dotterel plover considers her duty done when she has laid her eggs, leaving their hatching and the tending of the young to her mate. This trusting fellow will return to his parental duties shortly, even if a visitor settles down close to his abode; with patience he may be made to nest in one's hand. And the melancholic, flute-like call of the golden plover is a symbol of the mountains to all who love them. Incidentally, the dipper, which so much charmed Mr. Slingsby, has since been named Norway's national bird. This lively friend, found by brooks and rivers all the way up to the glacier's edges, is a sight to behold when making its dives into swift waters for food – even in the middle of winter. The bird may also be observed swimming under water, using its wings.

Of the reindeer this is to be said: Probably more were killed off by hunters than scared off by tourists. Anyhow, the reindeer now seen in the area are privately owned and looked after by herdsmen – though of the same stock as the wild deer. Only in the very western parts some deer may be considered ownerless; this is, however, a matter hotly disputed.

And on Slingsby's list are a number of species now extinct in the region, some practically extinct and others endangered: the bear (tracks last seen in Utladalen in the 1940's), the glutton (the European wolverine, systematically killed off during the 1950's), the lynx (occasional tracks and/or sightings are reported), the wolf (a whole century after its presumed extinction a lone animal was heard in Meadalen a winter's night, howling at the moon – a last greeting, the loner was killed somewhat further to the east), the eagle (very rare indeed). Add to this the polar fox, the horned owl, the large falcons, and the list becomes impressive – as well as disheartening to any conservationist. Yet, there is still hope that some of these species may survive or return and increase in numbers.

And, to bring in an optimistic note: The red deer, mentioned by Slingsby as an occasional visitor, must have been rare indeed; at that time this animal was almost extinct in Norway. But it has since greatly increased in numbers and today is found in all the woods of Jotunheimen. The elk (the European moose) is also numerous now, and may even be met above the timberline. And the roe has turned up in the area – in Lom first reported by a couple of children who were scared out of their wits, thinking they had seen the cattle of the supernatural "hulder" people! Now the species is fairly common.

And then there is the tentative return of the polar fox –.

Tales of Trout

Until recent years, before char and greyling had been introduced into some of the smaller lakes, "fish" in Jotunheimen meant one species only: trout. And many are the tales of the "big ones" of an earlier age. Thus goes one, related by a man from Lom: "My father and his friend Rolf were fishing in Hovde-

Fair-sized trout may still be caught by those who know where and how. This one was landed by Netoseter in Bøverdalen, and the fisherman is Eilev Slålien.

langtjønn. At dusk they caught sight of a big fish which by mistake had gotten into shallow waters. They jumped into the lake, grabbed him and threw him out. Rolf was a tall man, but when he carried *that* fish, hung from a branch on his shoulder, it reached all the way down to his knees."

And it is certain that very large trout have been caught in the area; in the fishermen's cabins by various lakes portraits of the biggest ones have duly been carved onto benches and tables.

But the trout did not make its way into Jotunheimen on its own; the rivers leading from the ocean to the mountain lakes have falls that it could not possibly pass. However, man may have offered his help as far back as in the Stone Age, carrying the fish past difficult stretches, and thus bringing along his dinner for years to come. This practice of setting out fish is still going on, although now in a scientific manner. And the trout is an adaptable creature.

Left, above: Irrigation has been used from time immemorial in Jotunheimen communities on the shady side of the mountains precipitationwise. Water from reliable sources was led by way of ditches and taken across gullies or depressions in the terrain in wooden troughs or by aquaducts built from rough stones (the latter especially in Årdal). The ditch between the road and the river in the picture is located at an altitude of some 1200 m in Sålell, Lom, and is part of a super-system carrying the water approximately 15 km to fields in the valley 800 m below. In recent years most of those systems have been replaced by automatic water sprayers. The one in the picture is, however, still in operation.
Below: Water spouts on lake Tesse. The winds off Heggjeberget are infamous, when they hit, it is a matter of getting to shore as fast as possible.

Only recently it has been realized that the variation of size, markings and colouring exhibited by the species, is a matter of nourishment and living conditions rather than inheritance: a brook trout, small and brownish, will become big and shiny if moved to a lake. In Jotunheimen, an area offering differing conditions from one lake to another, the fish vary as to size, shape and colouring. Also, trout will thrive at higher altitudes than has previously been realized – and a fellow who, for a joke, set out a couple of nets in Juvvatnet, at 1840 m, was pleasantly suprised when he caught splendid fish.

However, people of the area complain that the trout genereally is getting smaller and more scarce. And a few years ago at Sylvetjønn by Tesse, where trout weighing up to 14 kg have been caught, I saw 30 hopeful fishermen trying their luck without even getting a nibble.

The sport has become so popular now that it is necessary to protect the fish. Only fishing by rod, and that upon securing a licence, is allowed people who do not dwell in the area or own fishing rights.

But last year a chap from Heidal landed a couple of good-sized ones in – – – well, never mind where.

Talking about the Weather

From the western ocean storms move in, hurling themselves at the naked peaks of Hurrungane. Day upon day blizzards rage on the icy plateau of Sognefjell – weatherwise this is one of Norway's roughest spots.

However, in the Jotunheimen area, with high mountains and deep valleys, the prevailing winds, westerly summer and winter, show their true character mainly on the peaks. Elsewhere their direction and force is modified by local conditions, and wind direction conforms to the lay of the land.

A few general notes: In winter the mountains generate cold, and a wind often blows down the valleys; on warm summer days the winds tend to blow up those same valleys – except where cold is emitted by a glacier. More precipitation falls to the west of the watershed than to the east, more to the south of the mountains than to the north. And more falls on peaks than in valleys. Registered yearly averages range from 1261 mm (Fanaråken, alt. 2062 m and far west) to 470 mm (Elveseter, alt. 674 m, east of the watershed and north of the mountains). Winters are rough; temperatures may go down to 35°C below freezing – yet the mercury may nudge above the freezing mark, even on Fanaråken in January. Summer temperatures also are fairly low; average at an altitude of a 1000 m is about 11°C in July. But day temperatures of above 20° are not uncommon. Incidentally, temperatures, as a rule, fall as the altitude increases, some .6° to each 100 m. Also: winds generally increase with altitude, and so does the chance of fog.

But who frets? One good day in Jotunheimen, summer or winter, and all the miserable weather that can possibly be imagined, is forgotten.

Man and the Mountains

Vera Henriksen

The road comes to an end, vehicles can bring you no further – the trail takes over. An ancient trail, meandering along, humbly subject to the lay of the land; taking you across brooks and fields of mountain grasses, offering footholds on rock-strewn slopes, a track among the shrubs and heather.

To a wanderer bent on discovery, the trail has its own peculiar fascination, urging one on towards the view around the next bend and the un-known valleys between distant mountains. The trail has to become dear and familiar before one senses that it also offers its own kind of peace: the peace of meadows where tiny white and yellow blossoms nestle among grass covering the site of dwellings long abandoned – of footbridges crossing clear streams where trout glide shadowy over the sand and rocks of the riverbed – of late summer nights, when time seems to touch eternity as the white glow of glaciers reflects the moon's light.

This is an all-engulfing peace, giving meaning to experience itself.

And one's roots in the past, the bonds tying one to its men and women, become evident. One senses a timeless fellowship with those who, through the centuries, the millenia, have walked the paths of these mountains.

They saw the views we see; heard the rushing waters of the same streams, the roar of the same waterfalls. What did all this mean to them? Where did they come from, and what brought them here?

Prying out the Secrets of the Past

"Once upon a time", quite a few years ago, I began a quest to learn about those people and their way of life. The search was to bring me into contact with archeologists and historians, and with specialists in many fields. And it brought me into libraries and archives. It also brought me in contact with our time's dwellers of the Jotunheimen area and gave me new friends; eventually I made the area my home. And little by little I learned to recognize and interpret relics of the past: implements left by stone age man, archers' hideouts, reindeer traps, traces from the production of bog iron, lairs made by trappers of live falcons for the king's treasury –.

But I learned, also, that some mysteries of these mountains have never been unraveled. And one reason may be that the area has not been subject to a thorough archeological survey; lack of grants has limited excavations to more or less hurried jobs in areas about to be flooded by hydroelectric reservoirs. This does, however, mean that the possibility of making chance finds is fairly great, especially if one knows what to look for; a good many finds of significance have been made by observant people of recent times. But it is a matter of extreme importance that all such finds be forwarded to the archeological

Next page: The trail – how did it begin?

museums of Bergen or Oslo, with a note telling where the object was picked up (besides, according to Norwegian law finds dating from the Middle Ages and earlier, are the property of the government). This is so because each find is a piece of a puzzle that slowly brings out a picture of the past –.

But what then, is the extent of our present knowledge?

The Mists of Morning

The glacier of the most recent ice age was pulling back from the coasts of Norway between 10000 and 11000 years ago. Plants found nourishment in the barren soil – soon animals gained foothold, then man, the hunter. Reindeer were his main prey; the deer and their pursuers had followed the edge of the glacier as it withdrew through Northern Europe, and came to these shores only a few hundred years after the ice had left them free. As the glacier kept on dwindling, hunter and prey moved inland and, eventually, some 8500 years ago, reached the high mountain region. Habitation sites from that period have been located in mountain areas north and south of the Jotunheimen massif, but, strangely, not in Jotunheimen itself.

Reindeer, the prey of Stone Age hunters.

The heartshaped arrowhead below is fashioned from quartz. That, and the points below right, have been found in Jotunheimen. They are of uncertain age and may date from the latter part of the Stone Age, from the Bronze Age or Early Iron Age.

Those mountains seem as if shrouded in morning mists; in glimpses one discerns, through a haze, certain indications of man's presence. But no proof is given. And not until approximately the year 2000 BC does the fog disperse.

From that period and on a number of stone age habitation sites have been located, mainly in the eastern part of the region and on the shores of large lakes: Tesse, Vinsteren, Nedre Heimdalsvatn – Tyin being the only location west of the watershed –. People living here fashioned their implements from flint, slate and quartzite; flint is not native to the area, and must have been brought from the coast. No evidence of permanent housing has been found; one therefore presumes that the Jotunheimen people dwelt in tents made from animal hides. And they boiled their food by dropping heated rocks into the cooking utensils – rocks characteristically cracked by this procedure are found in connection with their dwelling sites, but no remnants of pots – they probably did their cooking in utensils of wood or hide.

It is taken for granted that they were reindeer hunters. It is also reasonably sure that they had boats and killed the deer as they were swimming, when they were most easy to get at. But, in addition, they must have known the reindeer's habits and its trails and stalked their prey on land. The most primitive of hunting methods, that of driving animals off the edge of a cliff, probably has been used in Jotunheimen, though no proof exists. A more advanced method, that of driving the animals towards a pass where archers and spearmen were in hiding, is known to have been used in the Årdal region even in historic times. Incidentally, a find made elsewhere in Norway proves the flint arrowhead to be an effective weapon indeed: one is still firmly entrenched in a reindeer vertebrae.

But here ends our fairly certain knowledge of these people.

However, the finds indicate that two different groups, both small in numbers, hunted in the area. Supposedly reindeer were not their only prey, and probably they caught trout which they had introduced into the Jotunheimen lakes. Furthermore, many archeologists believe that they were nomads, living

in the mountains part of the year only – the rest of the time roaming over a large territory, possibly ranging as far as to the coast.

But what was it like to be a Stone Age hunter in Jotunheimen? Only by giving one's imagination free reins, one may even attempt an answer.

Being constantly on guard, and watchfulness, may have been the main difference between their attitude and ours; they probably had a wariness that we associate with animals – a sensitivity to the least draught of wind, to smells, to sounds, to changes of light. While we tend to move like tanks through a landscape, experiencing mainly ourselves and our self-importance, Stone Age man must have moved quietly, observantly, being truly a part of his environment. A feeling of solidarity with his group probably also was part of his life, and necessary for his survival. And if we are to judge by the stone age peoples of our own times, then those skin-clad hunters of the past were in no way inferior to us, intellectually or emotionally – they knew the entire range of human feelings: anger and happiness, rage and tenderness, hatred, love, jealousy, friendship, envy, contempt –.

The story of Stone Age man is a separate chapter in the history of Jotunheimen. The relics he left prove his presence; his habitation sites are found on

Stone Age habitation sites have been located on the shores of several large Jotunheimen lakes. By Tyin archeologists worked under high pressure to beat the flooding of their sites as the water level of that lake, dammed for hydroelectric purposes, kept rising. The excavation site below, on Tyin's eastern shore, was under water only a few days after the picture was taken.

Mists enshroud Jotunheimen. Foreground (left to right) Gravdalstind, Storebjørn, Kalven and Saksa, the latter three part of the Smørstabbtindene group. In the background Gjertvasstind, Styggedalstind and Skagastølstindene.

windblown ridges near river outlets, or on a peninsula – maybe in close proximity to a big boulder. But he did not leave much behind. A layer of charcoal from a campfire may appear where waves have washed away part of some shore; cracked "boiling stones" are found, and chips of flint almost invisible among the gravel. If lucky, one may come across a scraper, a flattish stone chipped into shape by human hands, more seldom an axe, dagger or arrowhead. And stone weapons may be found wherever these people pursued their game. They are Jotunheimen's mysterious people. We know little of their origin and even less about their ultimate fate.

The mists once more enshrouds the mountains, staying there, seemingly impenetrable, throughout the "Bronze Age" and way into the "Iron Age".

Towards a New Way of Life

In order to bridge this gap in the history of Jotunheimen, I shall have to recapitulate briefly what happened elsewhere in Europe.

Approximately 3000 years ago the knowledge of iron had become widespread in south-eastern Europe (and the middle East), and that metal was substituting bronze as a main material for implements. However, in Norway bronze had never been of great importance, simply because the raw materials had to be imported. For a while stone held its own also against iron – until it became known that iron could ble obtained from a native source, the ore found in local bogs. This knowledge probably came to Norway from Central Europe, and archeologists believe that Norwegian bog iron production got under way some time between the years 500 and 400 BC. However, there is no definite proof of iron-making in Norway prior to the time of Christ.

PRE-HISTORIC
PERIODS IN NORWAY

Stone Age
abt. 10 000 BC – abt. 1500 BC

Bronze Age
abt. 1500 BC – abt. 500 BC

Early Iron Age
abt. 500 BC – birth of Christ

Roman Iron Age
birth of Christ – 400 AD

Period of Migrations
400 AD – 600 AD

Merovingian Period
600 AD – 800 AD

Viking Age
800 AD – 1050 AD

By then a people of farmers, arriving in Norway around the year 3000 BC, had settled on much of the best acre-land. And farming tools made of iron were a great improvement over those fashioned from stone. But for hunting stone weapons were still handy – and while the process of producing bog iron was labourious and slow, a suitable rock could be fashioned into an arrowhead or spearhead with relative ease. Most likely, therefore, iron and stone were in use simultaneously during one period.

Of Jotunheimen in this era of transition we know that the farmers gradually settled in valleys and by fjords bordering on the area – first (probably beginning in the Bronze Age, but with a main influx during the "Roman Iron Age") to the west and south; later (Merovingian period and Viking Age) to the east and north. And from those people seem to come the hunters who stalked in the mountains when iron came into use.

However, in Jotunheimen no find has been made bridging the gap between the Stone Age and the very earliest iron finds, of approximately the year 400 AD. This has caused much speculation, bringing forth several theories.

According to one, the Stone Age people continued to use the area uninfluenced by the development in the valleys – in which case there must have been either a conflict or practically no contact between the people of the mountains and those of the valleys. And several unsolved riddles present themselves: What happened to the Stone Age people later on? Did they die out or, maybe, were they killed off? Or did they themselves, in turn, become farmers, and, if so, where did they settle? According to another theory, farming changed the way of life so drastically that the mountains actually lay deserted during a long stretch of time. A third explanation has it that during this interim period the arrowheads were fashioned from bone, and therefore have withered away; this theory gets support in finds of bone arrowheads from early iron age in caves of western Norway.

Whatever the case may be, when the iron age came to Jotunheimen, it came to stay.

Bronze spearhead from Nord-Aurdal.

Of Iron and Gold

Most traces of Norwegian ironmaking have been found in the borderland between farms and mountains, some also in the mountain region. And several centres of bog iron production have been located in Jotunheimen.

We know quite a bit about this industry; much can be deducted from the finds. The method seems to have been identical with the one used in Iceland during the Viking Age and medieval times, and a skaldic poem gives a description of this procedure:

Early the smith must rise
if he is keen on riches;
harshly the bellows blow
fire into blue-black coals.

The sledgehammer bangs on gold,
red-hot slag spurts forth;
howling like wolves the bellows,
hissing the sputtering fire.

True, the skald, who was also a famed blacksmith, may have overdramatized somewhat. But the work certainly was strenuous, difficult and dangerous. And his use of the metaphor "gold" for iron aptly expresses the importance of this "gold of the bogs". The viking raids, and the revolution instigated by them of Norse society, were direct consequences of the possibility presented by the bog iron of domestic weapon production; it is not surprising that people of those times greatly admired their blacksmiths, even believing them to possess supernatural powers.

However, the poem demands a few words of explanation. Two raw materials were needed: bog iron ore and charcoal. Long rods were used to locate the ore in the bogs; the ore was then dug out, dried and crushed. Charcoal, necessary to generate sufficient heat, almost 1200°C, to melt the slag and thus separate it from the iron (with a somewhat higher melting point), was produced in a "coal pit", a primitive kiln. The main work took place in a furnace pit, a potshaped hole in the ground, up to 1 m wide and 35–65 cm deep. These pits were stone-lined, slabs frequently being used for the purpose, and had an inner lining of clay. There also was a "prefabricated" model, fashioned from burnt clay.

But in order to get a close look at the process, we shall now move back to the ninth century, and I shall put meat on the skeleton of existing theories by adding a little bit of fiction. However, a slab-lined furnace like the one I am going to describe, has been found by Øvre Sjodalsvatn. And a few kilometers away a ninth century grave with blacksmith's tools among the funeral goods, has been excavated. It could have happened just like this.

The mountain-sides by Øvre Sjodalsvatn seem to catch fire as the light of daybreak hits the birches' autumn foilage. But the little group on a ridge by the lake is too busy to notice; a blacksmith with a helper and two of his thralls

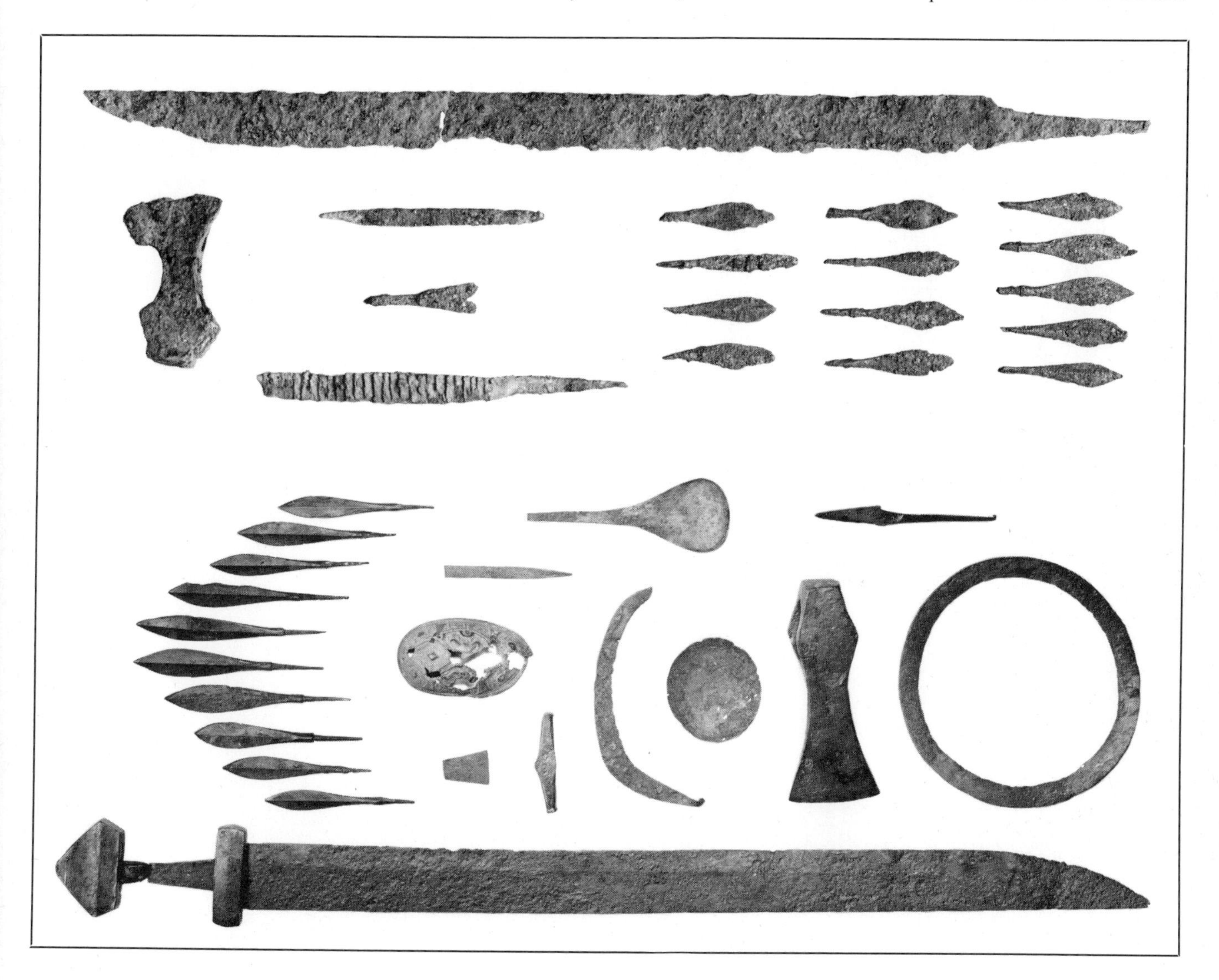

The upper part of the picture shows a Merovingian Period find from a grave by Bygdissundet, the sound connecting Bygdin with Raufjorden.
Below is shown the find from Griningsdalen in the Sjodalen region, one of the most extensive and remarkable Iron Age finds made in Norwegian mountains. A huntsman happened upon it in the year 1901 – a fox had its den in the burial mound, and iron implements protruded among the gravel. The find consists of, among other objects, a single-edged sword dating from the first half of the 9th century, arrowheads, an axe, a sickle, a strike-a-light, a hammer and an oval bronze brooch.

are gathered around a furnace pit. One thrall stands by the bellows, which lie on the ground and have a long clay nozzle leading into the pit. And the helper is kneeling by the furnace, pouring in hot embers from a soapstone vessel. The chips of wood in the pit catch fire, and the thrall slowly treads the bellows to kindle the flames. Some time is required to pre-heat the furnace; meanwhile the other men bring charcoal and ore. Then, at a signal from the smith, his helper starts shoveling charcoal into the furnace. And the smith sprinkles rust-coloured ore in between layers of coal, while muttering magic formulas.

The thrall gets busy with the bellows, and the noise of the fire is rising; even in the chilly morning breeze the work makes the man perspire. But the smith takes no notice of his thrall; he sits by the furnace continually murmuring his

Dispersing mists – Sjoa river.

formulas, ever more ardently watching the glowing mass. The exact moment when the slag begins to melt is of extreme importance – if the furnace gets too hot, the iron will be spoiled, and the margin between enough and too much is uncomfortably slim. The heat rising from the pit makes perspiration run down his face, too.

Time passes. The thrall at the bellows is gasping for breath now, and his pace is slackening. At last he is relieved by the other slave, and throws himself, panting, on the ground. The second thrall is worn out, too, when the slag is finally melting.

Below right: Furnace pit for production of bog iron. This one is from Møsstrand in the Telemark district and was used during the 8th century.

The smith raises his hand, and the bellows are moved more slowly – he works with the iron down in the sputtering, flaming mass, tries to collect it in the centre of the pit. The lump of metal grows, sinks; the slag swells. Even the thralls have their eyes riveted on the smith when, at last, he carefully lifts the glowing, pliant lump of iron out of the pit with a pair of tongs, and carries it to a big stone.

Then the sledgehammer strikes against hot iron, hits with viscious blows, by each spurts of molten slag are forced out of pockets where it has collected. The other men get busy removing the slag from the pit before it hardens; the helper curses as a droplet of slag from the iron hits him.

But the smith puts his sledgehammer aside and grips an axe, and with one blow almost splits the soft lump of metal. Then he smiles; it looks right. Later, in his smithy, he shall reheat it and hammer out more of the slag, before he considers it ready for use or sale.

We do not know how early iron production began in Jotunheimen; datable finds are few. Among the oldest is a key from the period of Migrations; it was found buried in a heap of slag near Beitostølen, and proves that iron was produced there at that time. We have a few chance finds, too, from that period: an arrowhead and a celt (a kind of axe shaped like a chisel) found in Veodalen, and an arrowhead picked up by an observant tourist in the year 1975, from the path between the Memurubu and Glitterheim lodges. A couple of finds, a spearhead from Hesthø by Memurubu and a dagger from Eidsbu by Bygdin, may be even older, dating back to the Roman Iron Age. From the Merovingian period there are several finds, among them an arrow-

Arrowhead from the period of Migrations (400-600 AD) found in Veodalen. Chance finds of arrowheads are fairly common.

head supposedly found at Galdhøpiggen – and the large burial find with blacksmith's tools mentioned above, from Griningsdalen in Vågå.

Throughout the Middle Ages a good iron bog was an excellent source of income, iron fetching high prices. The method of production remained fundamentally the same, though technical improvements were added: canals for draining off the molten slag, waterwheels to pump the bellows. However, in Jotunheimen this technical development ends in a mystery.

Not far from Randsverk are found the remnants of a first class set-up for bog iron production, practically a small industrial plant. A brook close to the furnace has been dammed, and below is timber for a hut housing a waterwheel, part of which has been found. Nearby a pit has been dug for a charcoal kiln, and there is plenty of ore. But there is neither charcoal nor slag, and one of the split logs hollowed out to conduct water, is only half finished. What could have happened; did the owner suddenly die? Or, possibly, was bog iron production outdated by the time this splendid plant was almost ready? For a time arrived, around the year 1600, when bog iron was displaced by iron from blast furnaces.

Yet, for a couple of centuries more, bog iron was produced to meet local demands. And in a book published in the year 1785 a local pastor strongly recommends that production on a large scale be resumed, being of the opinion that this would constitute a splendid source of income. Possibly the unfinished plant by Randsverk is a memorial to his unfounded optimism?

Anyhow, the last time bog iron is known to have been produced in the Jotunheimen area was in the year 1816 in Vågå. But relics of this industry of more than a millenium are legion.

Production generally took place near the summer farms. If the water of a bog in the vicinity of such a farm has an oil-like surface layer, and if, furthermore, rusty-red matter is found at the bottom of the creeks draining that bog, chances of finding traces of iron-making are great.

Most noticeable among these relics are the heaps of slag; some are huge, 2–3 m high and 20–30 m in circumference. But the shape varies; they may be oblong as well as round, or shaped like a horseshoe around the furnace. However, most are smallish and resemble ant-hills. And their soil, mixed with ashes, is quite fertile; juniper, especially, thrives on slag heaps.

The furnace pits, covered with overgrowth, are more difficult to locate – though I know people who have come across one unexpectedly. And finding the kiln is almost impossible without prior experience. An archeologist tells that even he had searched a site for one in vain, until he accidentally lost his footing, tumbled down a slope and found himself – sitting in the kiln.

The Trappers and the Archers

To people of communities bordering on Jotunheimen the mountains have been a huge store-room from which they fetched supplies of various kinds: meat and fish, and pelts for clothing, bed-covering and trading. To some men hunting has been a way of life; from as far back as the Migration period graves have been found with the burial goods consisting mainly of hunting and fishing gear. But to most people hunting was a secondary means of subsistence. Yet, in years when the crops failed, the bounty of the mountains was of vital importance to everybody.

Jotunheimen consequently abounds in hunting relics of past ages.

Well known are the hunters' stone huts, but not all of those are easily

In Heidalen around the year 1910. The picture is from the Wilse collection, Norsk Folkemuseum.

located, many having been built on rock-strewn land. I have looked for one in vain, even though I knew approximately where it was located. Such huts are ageless; any one may have been in use for a thousand years and more, but may also be of fairly recent origin. Dating them is impossible, unless one comes across an implement that dates or predates that particular hut to that particular object. The same goes for an even older type: lairs where shelter by a boulder or a cliff has been improved by human hand. Then there are caves, where people have sought refuge since the Stone Age.

The archers' hideouts and the reindeer traps (pitfalls) with their "guiding fences", are less known, but are found in great numbers.

The hideouts have stone walls, ½–1½ m high, usually forming a semicircle, and they are large enough for a man to crouch inside – some are partly dug in the ground. Generally they have been built in groups of up to 10–12, and are connected by stone walls. They are located near the reindeer trails, usually where those run through a narrow passage, for instance a notch. The largest (and, incidentally, at an altitude of about 1900 m also the highest) grouping of hideouts so far registered in Jotunheimen, is found by a notch in the Lomseggen ridge, about 5 km to the south-west of that mountain's summit. 82 hideouts have been located there; more may appear as ice and snow, having covered the area for centuries, keep melting. A longbow fashioned from yew also has been found in the area.

The Jotunheimen reindeer traps are rock-lined pits, a couple of meters long, 60–80 cm wide and 1½–2 m deep. When in use, they were covered with branches and camuflaged with moss and the like. They are situated directly in the deer trails and, like the archers' hideouts, most frequently where nature forms a narrow passway: in a notch, between a river and a steep cliff, on a ridge or a strip of land between two lakes. The "guiding fences" are low stone walls; even today tracks show that reindeer tend to follow such fences when feeding. A single trap may have four fences, one from each corner, forming a letter X. But usually the pitfalls are placed in a row, parallel to each other and connected by fences. In Jotunheimen most of these groups consist of less than 10 traps. But large systems also may be found. In Lom, in the region Veodalen–Hæranoshø-Smådalen, more than 70 traps have been registered in one system. A few people set out to have a look at that area not many years

Key from the period of Migrations, found near Beitostølen.

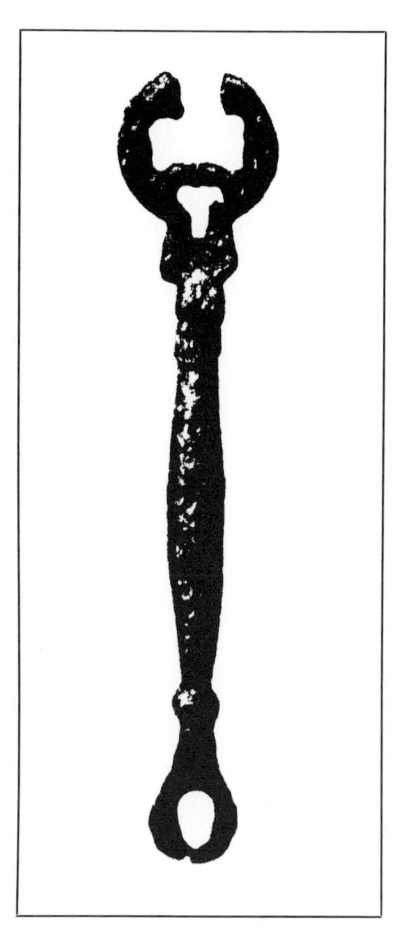

The author, by a reindeer pitfall in the mountain area between Veodalen and Visdalen. Below: Bergenussbua, Veodalen, has been used by drovers and huntsmen. Next page: Eidet, the strip of land between Bygdin and Tyin – hunting grounds of old.

ago, after having been told that there might be a couple of traps – our enthusiasm upon discovering what we had come across, may be imagined.

There are two theories regarding the way in which the traps were used. According to one, the owner camouflaged them, left and later returned to bring home his eventual catch. The other has it that deer were herded towards the pitfalls, where archers and spearmen also were waiting for the frightened animals. Both methods may have been used, possibly during different periods.

Dating these pitfalls and hideouts is just about as difficult as dating the stone huts. They may be ancient, some possibly of Stone Age origin. But in Jotunheimen we have indications only, as to their age, one being the above mentioned longbow of yew found in connection with a huge group of archers' hideouts. As to the pitfalls, the celt from Veodalen, also mentioned (Migration period) was found at the edge of one, thus making it very tempting to pre-date the pitfall to the celt. And one such trap of the nearby Rondane mountains has been carbon-14 dated (by help of organic material found in the pit) to shortly before the time of Christ; from a mountain area further south even earlier dates have been obtained. This does, however, give an idea only, of how old the Jotunheimen traps might be, and certainly proves nothing about the age of each particular trap. As a matter of fact, some may have been constructed as late as during the 18th century. A law was passed in the year 1730 limiting their use, but not forbidding it. And according to tradition, some were still in use during the 1800's. There is, for instance, the story of an Årdal huntsman (Johannes Hermundson Nundal, born 1815), who got into a quarrel with a fellow from Valdres about a deer caught in a pitfall near Tyin, in an area where people from Årdal and Valdres have fought from time immemorial over hunting and fishing rights. The Valdres man insisted that he owned the trap. But Johannes was not impressed; while patting his gun

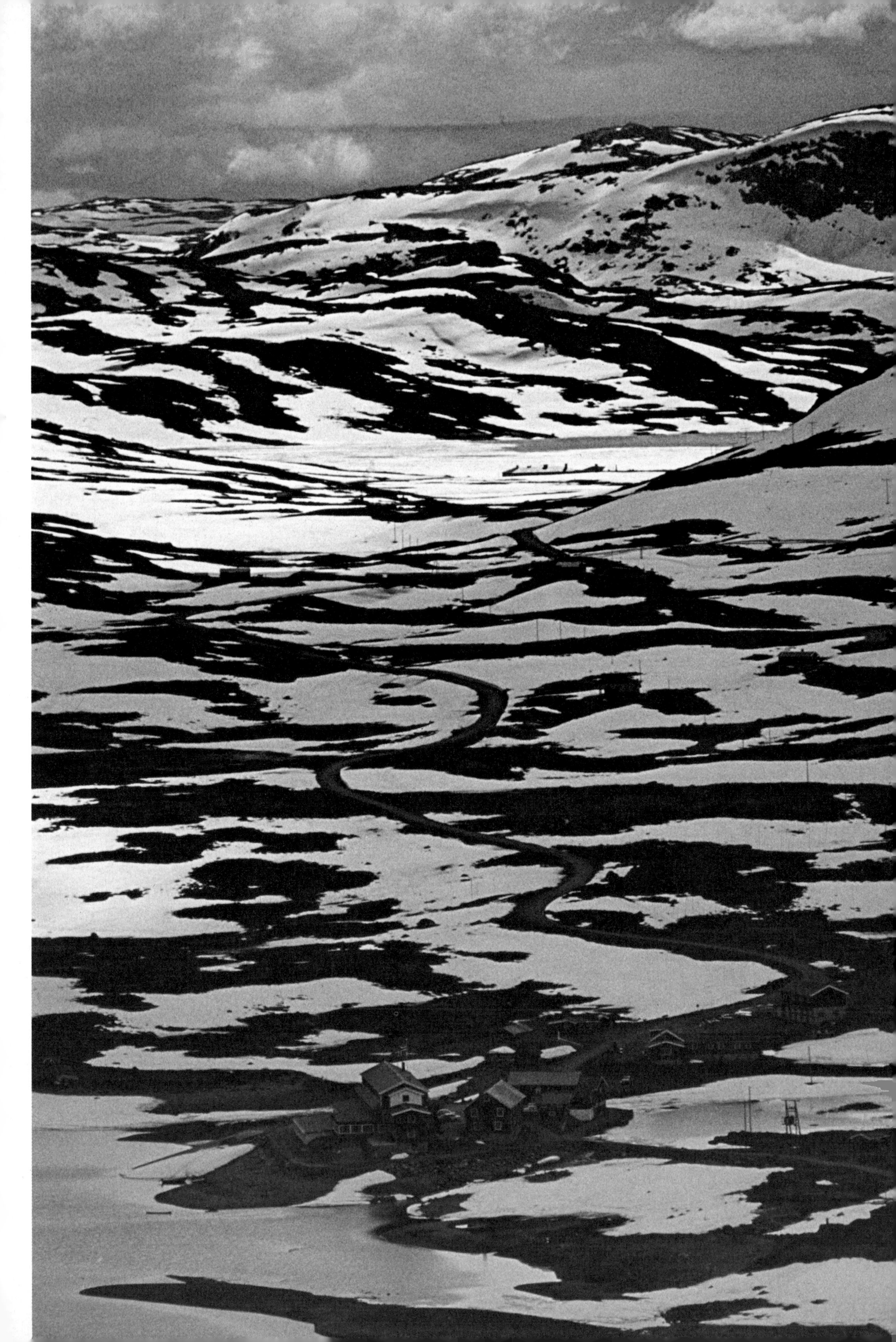

fondly, he calmly pointed out that "If you do not scram now, this old dear could hum a tune the like of which you have never heard.". The Valdres fellow prudently left.

Not until the year 1899 a law was passed which definitely forbids the use of the reindeer pitfalls – this being the last, but not by any means the first, time they are mentioned in Norwegian laws. Medieval laws show that single traps, or groups of them, were the property of individuals. But it is stated that "one who so wishes, may dig a trap in the commons (the mountains were considered as such) unless he thereby diminishes some other man's chance of making a catch." The law further states that no new pitfall may be dug so close to those belonging to another man that the blow of an axe is audible from one to the other – and this must have caused a few quarrels, in such cases people tend to hear what suits them. But the law thus limited the number of traps, keeping the deer from being taxed too heavily. According to traditions, the traps belonged to the farmers of nearby valleys. And a legend related to several farms in the area indicates how highly these pitfalls were valued: in one generation the farmer's oldest son is supposed to have chosen the traps in preference to the farm. Furthermore, we know from Valdres that a girl's attractiveness to prospective suitors was greatly enhanced if she brought as a dowry "traps in the mountains".

But reindeer was not the only prey in Jotunheimen. Just below the timberline is found a type of pitfalls larger than those intended for reindeer, and supposedly used for elk; a group of approximately a hundred of these is located in the Veoli-Hindseter area of Sjodalen. Other animals, marten, polar fox, hermelin and glutton, were hunted for their pelts. The polar fox is now practically extinct, but one may come across a deserted den (I once came *in* one, stepping through into it); in a sad way they may be considered relics of the past. As for the glutton: noblemen of an earlier age prided themselves in wearing the ragged skin of that animal; according to superstition a man sporting such a pelt would become as fierce and couragous as its original owner. And sleeping under a cover made from glutton skins was supposed to give the most tantalizingly uninhibited dreams. Anyhow, people of the Jotun-

Reindeer trap (pitfall) with "guiding fences". This one is found in the shade of Breikvamsnosi in Koldedalen by Tyin.

Showery weather, Storådalen. In the background, right, Semmeltind; the name is derived from "simle", "female reindeer", and is one of many Jotunheimen names bearing witness to reindeer hunting.

heimen area trapped the glutton with a special glee, since it was a rival reindeer hunter. And another, the wolf, was killed mainly as an enemy, its pelt, though readily used, was of minor importance. Bears were also hunted.

The snare probably is the oldest type of trap still in use. Otherwise the means of catching and killing animals have changed through the ages. A number of traps, more or less effective, have been used – iron was a prerequisite to the common-place, but cruel, toothed clamp traps, catching the animal by one foot; those have even been used for bears. The crossbow, an extremely effective weapon, precise, and forceful enough to shoot a quarrel through plate armour, came into use in Jotunheimen during medieval times; models with the bow fashioned from wood, horn and steel followed one another. But drawing a crossbow was quite a task, requiring a special tool; people therefore continued using the longbow where it was more handy, for instance for squirrel hunting. Still, it was faster to draw a crossbow than to load the guns that became known in the area during the latter part of the 16th century; that was an operation taking some 10 minutes. For hunting the crossbow also had other advantages over those guns: it was quiet, more accurate and weighed less. Guns were not commonly used in Jotunheimen until the second half of the 17th century; by then they were so much improved that their greater range made up for their disadvantages. But they were expensive, and cross-bows are mentioned in the area until the middle of the 18th century – an occasional one may still be found in the storage loft of some farm.

This means that bows were used for hunting well into modern times. And the first Jotunheimen huntsman known by name, Jahas Eldegard (born about the year 1600) from Årdal, certainly knew how to handle a crossbow, even if he used a gun in later years. Jahas became the patriarch of a clan numbering reindeer hunters in each generation during three centuries. And he has become a legendary figure not only as a huntsman, but for his reported friendship with the supernatural "hulder" people; it is said that when he played the jew's harp, they came out of their underground homes, dancing enthusiastically, their tails flopping. On one occasion, near Tyin, Jahas is even supposed to have shot a "troll" –.

However that may be, the famed huntsmen of ages past possessed a magnetism attracting to their names any number of legends. Of several it is even told that they "knew something", practiced witchcraft.

Thus, with these huntsmen and their guns an entirely different chapter about hunting in Jotunheimen begins: we leave archeology behind and enter the realm of tradition, legend and folklore.

Wielding a Gun

The next Jotunheimen huntsman that we know of, is Jakop Jensson, born in Valdres (Vestre Slidre) in the year 1663, and known as Bjødna-Jakop, Bear-Jakop. He was one supposed to "know something". His gun had been two years and a day in the making, being forged on three Good Fridays, and had a bore so large that 2 ounces of lead went into each bullet. An animal wounded by one of those was paralyzed, and Bear-Jakop could throw a spell on the game, compelling it to come within shooting range. Many a legend concerns his marksmanship; he is one of several of whom it is said that he has killed three reindeer with one shot. His hunting grounds in Jotunheimen was the Bygdin-Vinsteren area – and he hunted bears, even on Valdresflya.

Another huntsman from Valdres (Vang), known as a character as well as for his skill, was Finnkjell in Kjørlien (Kjørlien being his farm); his period of fame was the first half of last century. Finnkjell was on friendly terms with the hulder people, especially the girls – he was a good-looking man, and not one to chase a pretty girl away, even if she had a tail. One of his hulder girl friends taught him a lot that other people did not know about reindeer. Another, having spent a Saturday night with Finnkjell, promised that he should shortly get a chance at shooting deer. And on Sunday morning, when he opened the door, three large bucks were feeding near by. But Finnkjell did not touch his gun; he knew that it was sinful to shoot on a Sunday – and there were limits to what a good Christian might get himself into! Finnkjell's favorite hunting grounds were the mountains north of Bygdin, and his favorite place a hut by Galdeberg. Like many a huntsman, he was a poor farmer; when the urge to hunt came upon him, he ignored his farm and left for the mountains. In the end he sold Kjørlien and settled on a small patch of land, part of his former property. He was generous to a fault, and in his old age was reduced to stark poverty.

Regarding early huntsmen from north and east of Jotunheimen, most is known of Vågå and Heidalen. Hunters from those parts were renowned for extraordinary strength even more than for their marksmanship, they were big men who showed their mettle in a fistfight. Tales about their hunting concern mainly their fights with contenders and their ability to carry heavy loads.

Tjøstol Kleppe, the older of a pair of huntsman brothers, was born in Vågå in the year 1694. The younger, Ola, may have been the better hunter; he made a fair living from hunting and fishing, a feat not managed by very many in modern times. Once he shot 14 grown reindeer bucks in a week's time. But Tjøstol was stronger – and therefore gained more fame.

Another of these strongmen, Hans Heringstad (Big-Heringstad), came from Heidal and was Strong-Tjøstol's junior by about 30 years. He is known mostly for his successful fights with men from Valdres, over hunting rights in the Valdresflya area – he gladly took on a dozen of them, if they had the pluck to challenge him. In later years he admitted that he once, in a fit of temper, had killed a man, hiding the corpse somewhere in the mountains. A story is told about his shooting that is unusual in showing the hero in a rather unfortunate light: In Murudalen Hans came upon a bear eating the carcass

The hulder – man's dream of woman incarnate in a beautiful girl. Maybe she is still walking Jotunheimen's trails –.

of a cow. He took aim and fired, but the bear, a huge beast, jumped up and fled. Hans re-loaded his gun and set out in pursuit, caught up with the animal and fired at it once more – still without making a kill. And now the bear chased Hans, who struggled to load his gun while on the run. He managed that feat, turned and made a third try – upon which the bear ran first with Hans as the pursuer. Thus it went, back and forth, until the fifth bullet finally finished off that bruin.

It is beyond doubt that Jahas, Bear-Jakop, Finnkjell, Strong-Tjøstol, Big-Heringstad and a number of other legendary huntsmen are historical. What to make of the colourful tales told about these men, is an entirely different question; history in the usual sense of that word they certainly are not. Yet they convey one kind of truth: the truth about people's thoughts, daydreams and beliefs – reflected in their attitudes to the strange wilderness that Jotunheimen beyond the summer farms and beaten paths must have been to the ordinary valley dwellers. The huntsmen were different, and part of that world, near and yet so far removed that it seemed beyond the clergyman's domain. Here trolls and hulders held sway, one had to stay on friendly terms with them or keep them at bay. Even the stories of Big-Heringstad's fights with the Valdres men have some of the characteristics associated with the lore of trolls and hulders – especially a tale about a Valdres wedding feast, from which he barely escaped with his life –, and the account of his bear hunt is reminiscent of jocular folk-tales. Tradition indicates that quite a few of the Jotunheimen huntsmen have relished in their popular image of being special, and have played the part to the hilt. Even huntsmen of recent years have nourished the legend by telling tales from the borderland between truth and fiction. Here is one dating from the first decade of our century and told by Torkjel Øy of Lom:

It happened on one of the Memuru glaciers towards the end of a warm summer; the ice was wet and slippery. Torkjel shot a buck, but the animal slid down the shiny slope of ice and disappeared in a deep crevasse. Torkjel lost his footing and was heading the same way whem, at the last moment, he managed to drive his knife into the ice for a handhold. And he pulled himself up as far as possible. There he was, on a slippery slope with no hold for hand or foot, other than the handle of that knife – and below him the crevasse. His one and only chance of survival was to remain motionless until his buckskin breeches froze and stuck to the ice – then he cautiously pried loose his knife, drove it in for a new handhold further up, got his breeches loosened and pulled himself up a little, waited till his breeches again were stuck – and so on, until he could gain a sure footing!

But even if the huntsmen of old may have been masters of the joke and the tall tale, one matter was deadly serious to them: hunter's luck. And they were keenly aware of good and bad omens. The hoarse cry of a raven was a

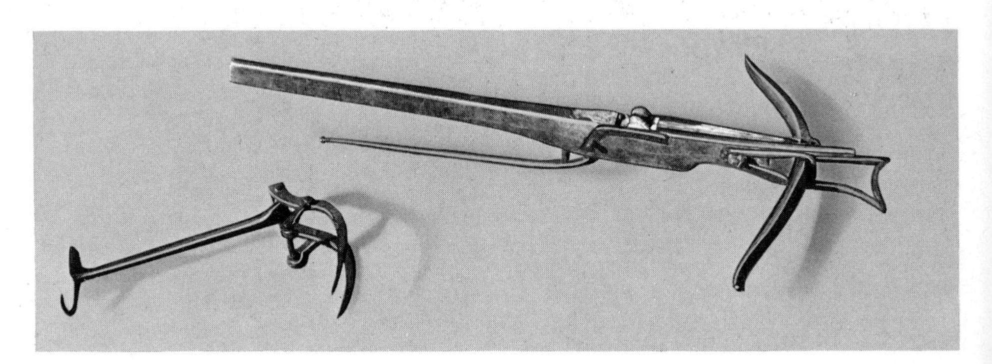

Crossbow (steel bow) with device used for drawing the string.

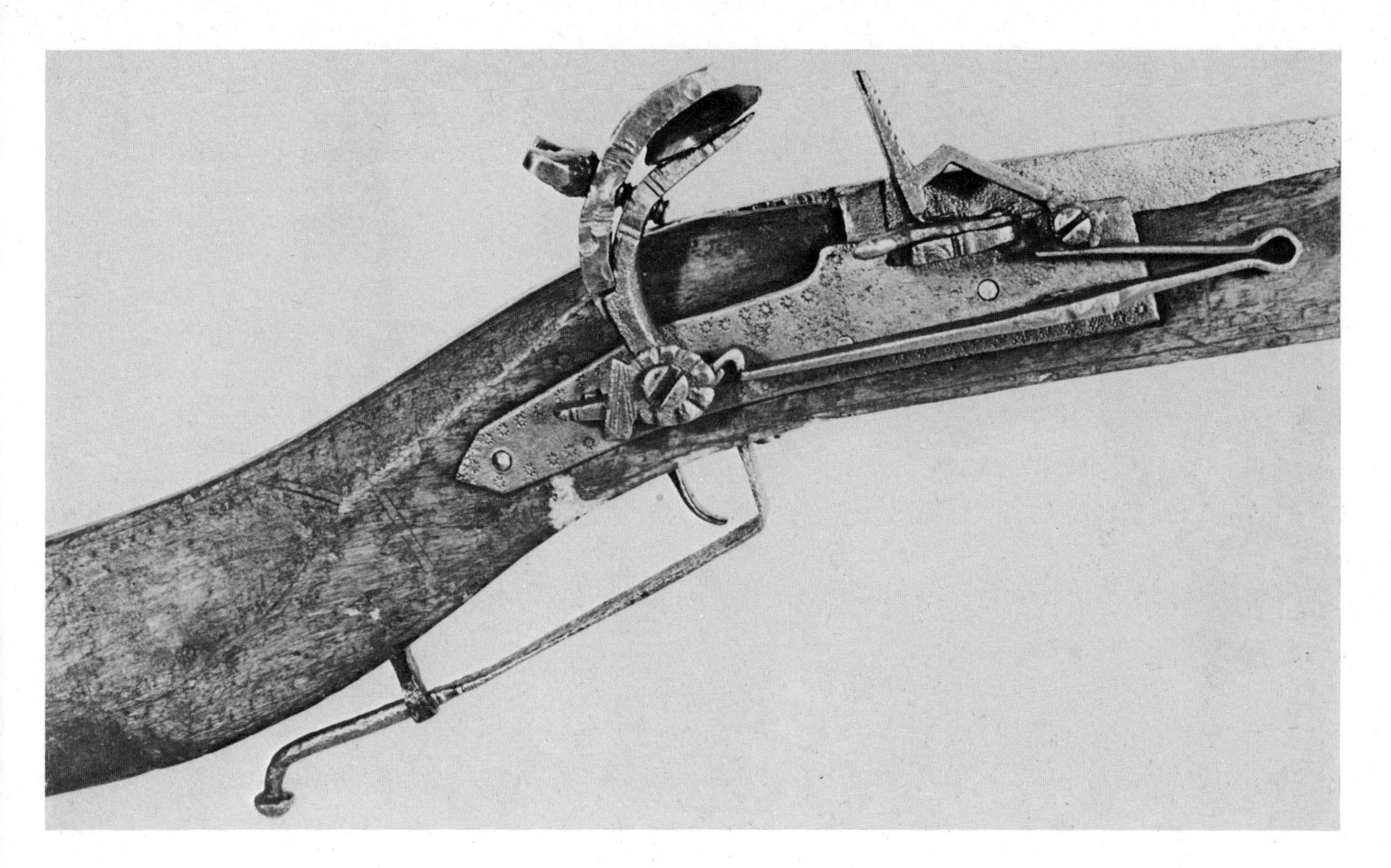

Snaplock gun; the snaplock was an early type flintlock, and flintlock guns were in use from the 16th century onwards, but chiefly during the 17th and 18th centuries. Even the snaplock variety was in use as late as in the 1700's. The lock had a flint fixed in the cock (hammer) that, on striking the battery of the pan, ignited the priming, which communicated its fire to the charge through the touchhole. While originally issued to the armed forces, the snaplock/flintlock guns were used for hunting by Norwegian farmers. Precursors to the flintlock guns (and also used contemporary with those) were the matchlock gun with a slowmatch igniting the charge, and the wheel lock gun in which the charge was ignited by sparks struck from a flint or a piece of iron by a revolving wheel.

promising sign, but meeting a woman of ill repute was so bad that one might as well go home. A number of superstitions concerned guns. Some men were suspected of ruining the weapons of others by means of magic – a remedy for this was to heat the gun barrel until the metal was red-hot. But most of those guns were notoriously unreliable anyway, and a reliable one was a friend for life to the old-timers. The story goes that Bear-Jakop, when he was very old and too weak to carry his beloved gun, still kept dragging it along, tied to a strap. And a ritual that may date back to pagan times, is that of drinking blood from the throat of the freshly killed buck – this was practiced in Jotunheimen as long as reindeer were stalked there, and in our century was lamely explained away with prattle about nutritional value. However, the practice is mentioned also in a book of the 16th century; the explanation there given is that this blood infused the hunter with the animal's savagery, strength and keen senses.

And no doubt the hunters of old needed strength and keenness, if not exactly savagery. Their guns were heavy, the hunt strenuous in the extreme, and carrying the catch home was a job that might kill a man – it is said of Strong-Tjøstol that he once carried a fully grown reindeer buck, a load of well above a 100 kg, up the steep and narrow Besseggen ridge. They also had to do without a lot of equipment that is considered indispensable nowadays: matches, sleeping bags, rain-wear, binoculars, compasses –. The strike-a-light used to make fire consisted of flint, steel and tinder, kept in a leather pouch. This contrivance could be temperamental, and one had to take care that no spark was left in the tinder when returning it to the pouch – no lesser man than Bear-Jakop once felt his pocket getting uncomfortably hot. The only kind of sleeping bag known, was the bloodied reindeer hide that a man might bundle up in if caught in a blizzard; many a man is supposed thus to have saved his life. Even the lack of such a minor piece of equipment as sun glasses might be fatal: snow blindness could render a man helpless. And the standard

Tesse. Nordseter in the foreground. By this northern shore of the lake are found pitfalls that, according to tradition, have been used to trap elk.

procedure to avoid this, smearing soot around one's eyes, did not always help. Of hunting during winter there is, furthermore, this to be said: people had to make their own skies, which was a difficult job – a story about a famous huntsman who lived in Kvikne in the 18th century, Anders Masseng, rather dramatically illustrates that: He and a couple of other men had been chasing a bear out of its winter lair, the animal went for Anders, with one blow tore part of his scalp loose and left it hanging in front of his face. "The trolls take him!" said Anders when he had wiped the blood out of his eyes, and the bear was killed. "He broke one of my skies!"

Except for hunters' huts dated by local tradition to within the last 150 years, the gun huntsmen have left few relics in Jotunheimen. Here and there one may notice that stones have been moved aside to make a deep hollow in a rock-strewn slope, and that the place is marked with cairns. Such hollows were used by hunters as temporary store-rooms for meat, which was carefully covered with rocks to keep the birds and beasts out. These storage places may have been used once only, or time and again through a long period. In the pass between Austabotn and Gravdalen in Årdal one of exceptional size is found: 3 m long and 1 ½ m wide. And close by is a group of 13 archers' hideouts. Which brings us back to archeology.

But no find of any kind is necessary to establish a feeling of contact with the huntsmen of old. There are reindeer in Jotunheimen still, even if they are free game no longer. The deer still move upwind in the bright days and pale nights of summer; still the squeeky noise from hoofs may be heard, still the deer kick snow off the windblown ridges of winter in search of food. And one may still stop short, breathless, at the sight of a group of large bucks, magnificently crowned with heavy antlers.

The Fish Hunters

The old Norse word "veiða" means to fish as well as to hunt; a "veiðimaðr" was a man who made his living by both. And the earliest evidence of fishing in the Jotunheimen region comes from graves dating back to the period of Migrations: a "veiðimaðr" is buried with his leisters and fishing spears as well as his hunting equipment. But we shall never know exactly when fish were introduced into the various Jotunheimen lakes – this has been a gradual process, probably beginning in the Stone Age, and still going on.

The earliest written record, and a fairly unusual one, is a runic inscription carved into a stone approximately 1050 AD: "Eiliv Elk carried fish into Raudsjøen". What Eiliv pointed out in such a durable manner, presumably was that he thereby had secured the fishing rights to that lake for himself and his descendants. The distance from Raudsjøen (in Gausdal) to Jotunheimen is short, and most probably the same practice regarding fishing rights was common there. And medieval parchments show the value of those rights by documenting that the owners of some farms in the Jotunheimen area possessed such rights. From the 16th century records show that a number of farmers paid their taxes in fish.

The fish, always trout, was caught in nets, by hooks, with leisters and in various kinds of traps. The right, not only to lakes, but to favourable spots, were jealously guarded and, like the reindeer pitfalls, highly regarded as dowry. The importance of the catch is further underscored by the constant quarrelling going on about these rights; quarrels attested to through the centuries by documents ranging from a testimonial with the king's seal appended, to a subpoena of the year 1667, of two men of Øystre Slidre in Valdres, who had smashed the boat of a third party. By Tyin, men supposedly even have killed for the sake of fishing rights. There is, however, a rather amusing discrepancy between the evidence thus given of the value of the catch, and the figures appearing in old tax rolls. According to one such, of the year 1663, not a single farmer of Vang in Valdres, a district counting among its assets a great number of lakes teeming with fish, for instance the famed Tyin, admitted to having the least bit of income from fishing!

A feature of fishing, as well as of hunting, was the great number of superstitions flourishing. One way of gaining fisherman's luck was to eat the

Sinker of a type probably used on fishing nets. A number have been found on the shores of Tesse when that lake has been tapped to below normal water level – as was this one, photographed in situ.

heart cut from a live fish. And crosses galore were carved onto the fishing gear; people even drew the sign of the cross in the water before setting a net. Furthermore: a hook that a fisherman had kept hidden under his tongue while going to communion, would always infallibly bring in a catch.

Chance finds of old fishing gear in Jotunheimen are rare. Lines and nets were perishable, whether they be fashioned from horse-hair, goat's hair or flax. And as the equipment has hardly changed during the ages, eventual finds are seldom datable. However, sinkers for nets have been found in lakes that periodically are tapped below their normal water level. A type from Tesse looks like a small wheel; one has been carbon-14 dated to Viking Age.

But it is unlikely that the average tourist should chance upon one of those. More visible testimony to Jotunheimen's history of fishing and quarrelling are the fish traps, still to be seen in brooks and rivers – here and there a row of stones standing on end, those have been used when the nets were spread out to dry – and then the fishermen's cabins, or building sites showing where they once stood.

But in calm summer evenings rising trout break the mirror surface of mountain lakes –.

Summer farming – a Relic of Nomadism?

Three theories are current regarding the origin of summer farming. One states that cattle led the way to mountain areas in seach of better pastures. A second sees the beginning in a nomadism going back to pre-farming times in this country. And according to the third, summer farming was part of the way of life of a people settling in Norway during the Stone Age. Possibly no single theory gives the complete answer; summer farming is, however, undoubtedly an ancient phenomenon. Medieval laws mention the practice, saying that it goes back to "days of old"; the old Norse word for summer farm is "sætr", modern Norwegian "seter". And in Jotunheimen graves from the Merovingian period as well as the Viking Age have been found near seters.

Farms in the Jotunheimen area usually had two seters, one relatively close to the homestead, and in use a couple of weeks each spring and autumn, the other, the summer seter, further away, up to 50 or 60 km – some people from Vågå have seters by Øvre Sjodalsvatn; Lom people have had theirs by Gjende –. In addition there have been "in-between"-seters, seters for resting, seters used in autumn only, and special goat-seters.

In the northern parts many summer farms were used in winter as well; this has been the case in Heidal, Lom and, especially, in Vågå. And the purpose of the winter sojourns in the mountains was to spare the trouble of hauling to the valleys fodder stored in the seter barns. From Vågå people and cattle left around All Saint's Day and stayed till Candlemass, and travelling could be rough if the weather turned nasty. Large seters, the size of small farms, bear witness to this custom, which is of uncertain age.

However, Jotunheimen also has a number of abandoned seter sites. There were various reasons why people moved away; maybe firewood was scarce in the area, or there was a danger of landslides. And then there has been the ebb and flow of social change through the ages. A number of seters as well as farms were abandoned after the great Plague of the 14th century, the Black Death – new ones were built and more added as population again increased. A maximum, with optimal use of the mountain pastures, occured during the 19th century – before the great waves of emigration to the United States,

Above: Spiterstulen in Visdalen abt. the year 1890 (photo by K. Knudsen, Bergen). To the right Skogadalsbøen in Utladalen abt. 1880 (photo by Axel Lindahl). Spiterstulen by that time had been enlarged to accommodate tourists. Except for that, the two seters are representative of the types used in the eastern (Spiterstulen) and western (Skogadalsbøen) parts of Jotunheimen. And a stone hut is not necessarily drafty; a well-constructed one has double stone walls, the in-between space filled with earth. Neither Spiterstulen nor Skogadalsbøen are seters any more. Presentday Spiterstulen offers to its guests comfortable quarters indeed, and Skogadalsbøen is one of the Norwegian Tourist Association's major lodges.

followed by the "flight to the cities", caused a marked population decrease in the region. Presently summer farming is again on the upsurge, but a new pattern is developing, based on the arrival of roads, tractors and trucks.

Housing on the seters has run its own course of development. Originally a cave may have served the purpose, maybe a primitive stone or wooden hut partly dug in the ground. The cattle was kept outside, in pens, at night. Eventually barns were built, and the main house got two or three rooms. But seter houses in general have been more primitive than those of the valleys; they were, as a matter of fact, frequently old houses moved to the mountains when they had served their time at the homestead. And innovations such as wooden floors and chimneys, came to the seters belatedly. However, the construction method and layout of the seter houses vary from one Jotunheimen area to another. Most noticeable: west of the watershed old seter houses are built of stone – lately wood is taking over –, while to the east log cabins are the rule, unless hauling the timber in would mean a great deal of trouble, in which case stone has been used.

Seters usually lie in clusters, forming small communities. In earlier times this was a matter of safety in numbers – wolves and bears roamed the mountain areas, as did occasional bands of robbers. But from lone seters, close enough to the valley community for a "lur" (Norwegian version of the Alpenhorn) to be heard, the girls in charge are supposed to have called for help by playing an agreed upon tune, in case robbers attacked.

Snow, sled, the man's clothing and the venerable log walls suggest an old-time seter in winter. The picture shows the stop-over (resting) seter at Randsverk, where people took a well-deserved break during the long trip from homestead to the seter of their destination. The house in the background does, however, indicate a rather recent date for the photo. And it was, in fact, taken in connection with a TV-program about the now obsolete practice of spending 2-3 winter months at the seters. So was the picture on the next page.

Livø Grev Øien showing how to make "skjørost", a Norwegian variant on the theme of cottage cheese. In course of the operation the soured milk is heated twice, and each time the curds are strained from the liquid, finally being kneaded together to make the cheese. Shown here is the second straining process.

The seter people tried to scare away four-footed beasts with noise and fires – even in our century a girl at Vormeli in Utladalen had to light torches to chase a bear. Traps were used, too. And if wolves got too aggressive, large numbers of hunters banded together to rid a whole region of those animals. Several might join, too, in killing a bear. Old bear-hunters' spears are still to be found on some of the farms. The men who used them, kneeling with the weapon held at an angle and supported on the ground, while egging the bear on – those men must truly have had ice water in their veins.

Woman's Work – in the Mountains

A number of portraits, written, drawn and painted, were made during the 19th century, depicting pretty seter maidens who might, just occasionally, milk a cow or a goat, but generally seem to have spent their time enjoying the sunshine and the scenery, blowing tunes on the "lur", melodically calling their cattle home, receiving handsome suitors from the valleys on Saturday nights

– and cooking for tourists enthusiastic about their "discovery" of Jotunheimen. Such pictures are, to put it mildly, misleading.

The girls undoubtedly might be good-looking and their suitors handsome. And dancing and fun could be part of seter life. Also: some of the women and girls welcomed the change offered by their stay in the mountains. But seter life first and foremost was a lot of hard work.

The Norwegian word for the woman or girl in charge on a seter is "budeie", implying that she is responsible not only for the welfare of the cattle, but for the dairy products of the important summer season, a large share of the annual yield of the farm. Consequently many a farm-wife stayed on the seter herself (in Valdres this has been and still is the rule), and the suitor turning up on weekends was her husband. Alternatively, a grown daughter or a daughter-in-law took charge. But the professional "budeie" also existed; she was highly respected and knew her own worth. In the autumn, when the budeies returned from the seters, special services were held in the churches in their honour, and from Lom we have an account of the budeie's return to the farm after a successful summer: "She was received as a highly honoured guest and treated to the choicest foods, while being conversed on seter life and local news. Then mother took her to the store-house where the summer's yield of dairy products was neatly stacked on the shelves. And the budeie rejoiced, to see that all had arrived undamaged – mother then formally thanked her for discharging her responsibilities in the best manner possible."

How, then, was everyday life on a seter?

Deserving mention, since they were part of the budeie's life in a matter-of-fact way hard to imagine nowadays, is the hulder people. They were there always, and were believed to take possession of the seter houses when the ordinary people moved out. However, they seldom caused trouble if one observed the established rules and rituals. One must, for instance, begin the summer's stay at the seter by addressing them; in Vestre Slidre (Valdres) the formula used was this: "We are going to stay here for a while, but if someone else is here, we are not going to bother you in any way." Tales of budeies and hulder women giving each other a helping hand are common – the general impression is one of congenial neighbourliness.

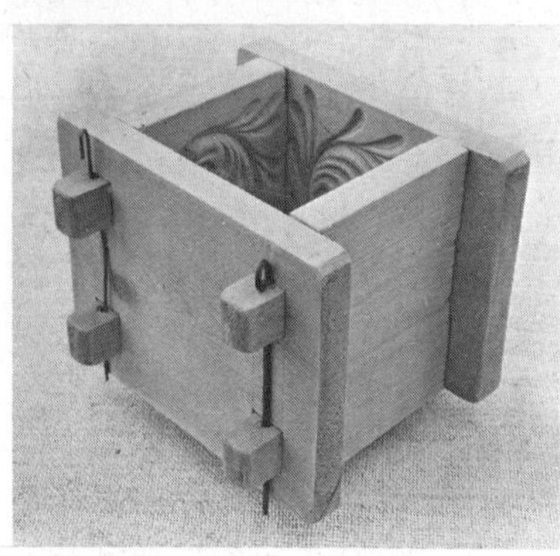

Tools for seter work. Above: hand-cranked cylinder churn for making butter from cream. This type (the one in the picture comes from Rusli, Vågå) is a relatively newfangled device, which came into use at the seters in the middle of the 19th century – the older type is a narrow, vertical vessel that was worked with a plunging dasher. Below: Cheese mold from Kampen seter (Vågå).

The budeie's work fell into three main categories. First, there was the care of the animals: cows, goats, sheep, frequently also swine. Milking took place mornings and nights; in times past the sheep as well as the cows and goats were milked. Where herders were not employed, as for instance in the Årdal region, the budeies took turns at that job. And in the evenings the animals were called home – which took time, even if the tunes used were lovely –. Second, there was the production of butter and cheese. When the budeie had milked, she poured the milk into bowls, each kind of milk into its own, lining them up on shelves in a special store-room; she had to take care that the contents of each bowl was used at the right time. Cheese-making, done in huge kettles, was an exacting and time-consuming task. A number of different kinds of cheese was made, and on many seters cheese-making took place every day, or, if herds were large, even twice daily. Butter was churned by hand once or twice a week. The third part of the job was that of keeping the various utensils scrupulously clean. In days of old those were generally fashioned from wood; every day a large number of them had been used and were thoroughly scrubbed. And cleaning the cheese-making kettle was a major job that had to be tackled after each use.

Next page: A worthy representative of seter women, Kaia Gjendine Slålien. This picture was taken in the old seter house at Gjendebu when she was 97 years old. She has told the story of her birth in that house: "In the year

(Continued)

1871 on May 30th my mother and father travelled to Gjendebu from Bøverdalen with 6 cows and 60 goats. ...On July 14th, in the evening, when my mother had finished milking, she told my grandmother that she was too unwell to return to the valley. Grandmother got frightened and fled to a cave where she hid until noontime the next day. Mother had to take care of everything alone. I was born at 4 o' clock in the morning..." When Gjendine was 17 years old, Edvard Grieg, visiting Gjendebu, heard her clear, musical voice as she was calling her cattle home in the evening. The result: his opus 66, "19 previously unpublished Norwegian folk-songs".

In addition came cooking and house-cleaning; if the farm-wife stayed on the seter, she brought her children and had to look after them. There were work-hands to feed in connection with various kinds of seasonal work: haying, taking moss for fodder, or cutting peat (common in the Fortun region) – the budeie often gave a hand to that work too. Then there was the gathering of fire-wood; large quantities were needed for the cheese-making, and finding enough could be a problem – the menfolk usually brought a load up on weekends when they came with pack-horses to fetch the produce. In some districts, for instance by Vinsteren, the budeies also caught and cured fish.

And generally they had needlework and other handwork to do: making shirts, knitting gloves and stockings, spinning – the distaff was used on the seters long after the spinning wheel had taken over in the valleys. Furthermore, many a budeie prided herself in bringing home exquisite embroidered pieces.

It seems obvious that her work-day, beginning at 4 or 5 AM, lasted until late at night. That the work did not necessarily dampen her spirits is proven by this story, from Vågå in the 1860's: During the moss-taking season, one of the work-hands was the kind of man who likes to play practical jokes on others, but hates to be the butt of them. The young budeie and the herder, a girl, both enjoyed teasing him. One morning his knap-sack seemed rather heavy, which he would not admit until discovering that the budeie had put a stone in with his lunch. He swore revenge and talked his helper into joining him. In the evening they locked the girls out from the seter-house in the chilly autumn air, lit a formidable fire in the fireplace and settled down to enjoy themselves. However, they did not stay put for long. The girls had plugged the chimney and locked the door from the outside – and windows of those days were not made to be opened. The fellows wheezed and coughed, their eyes smarting, while the girls outside were the ones having the fun. And the men had to solemnly promise not to take revenge, before that door was opened –.

Nowadays milk-trucks traffic the seter roads, the mountain meadows are mowed for ensilage, and the budeie might be a student on a summer job. As for the various utensils of old-fashioned seter work – those fetch sky-high prices in the city antique shops.

Interior of Gjendeboden, popularly known as "Gjendinebua", "Gjendine's hut".

Guridalen seter in the upper part of Utladalen is interesting not only as a typical western Jotunheimen seter. The first tourist to venture into Jotunheimen in winter, the British mountaineer William Cecil Slingsby, and with him two men from Fortun, skied from Helgedalen through the Keisaren pass to Guridalen in the year 1880 (page 144).

Gathering Moss

In times passed moss was a common supplement to other kinds of fodder, and has been used in Jotunheimen communities east of the watershed. 5–6 sleighs full for each cow was the average; large farms might use several tons.

Moss was taken between the haying and harvesting seasons or in the autumn, and was frequently gathered in the vicinity of the seters. Several kinds of moss and lichen were used, being collected in piles, each of a suitable size to be loaded on a sleigh, then left to freeze and be fetched when there was snow on the ground. Stacking each pile was an art; it had to be firm all through, and the surface so smooth that the winds could not scatter the moss – a long pole with the owner's name or seal made the finishing touch.

The moss gathering might go on for a couple of weeks and the whole household take part; frequently tenant farmers were obliged to come along. And fetching the moss-piles home in winter could cost lives if the weather suddenly took a turn for the worse. Yet, in its own way it must have been very special when, as I have been told from Vågå, horse-drawn sleighs in a long file came across Vågåvatnet in the blue dusk of a winter evening, the men riding high on their moss-loaded vehicles and singing.

In Jotunheimen one might still occasionally come across such a pile of moss, forgotten when that type of fodder lost out to concentrates.

The Drovers

Probably, cattle was herded to town and sold as meat-on-the-hoof even in medieval times. But proof of the practice is not given until the 16th century, when the accounts of the lord of Akershus (the castle of Oslo) show that cattle was thus herded from Gudbrandsdalen. During subsequent centuries this traffic increased; eventually large flocks were herded to the mountains to feed there during the summer, then, in the autumn, to town for sale. Inevitably a conflict arose between drovers and seter owners, over grazing rights; the ensuing legal battles are recorded in a large pile of documents.

The above pictures are from a pamphlet published by the Institute for Folklore Research (Institutt for folkeminnegranskning) in Oslo in the year 1969. Left: Pål Mo shows how, in Sjodalen in his youth, he took moss for fodder. Right: This is how hay is still carried into the barn at Kampen seter.

Droving and cattle trading became a way of life. In winter the traders travelled from one community to another, negotiating for cattle and horses; upon finishing a deal, a down payment was made, and the seller kept the animal until the drover came back for it. The traders travelled far and wide, generally making the same rounds every year. And towards midsummer they gathered the cattle and horses into droves and set out for the mountains. There were regular drovers' trails. One followed Moadalen up from Årdal to the pastures by Tyin, another went east from Fortun, crossing the 1500 m high Keisaren pass and continuing towards Tyin and Bygdin. Others again went south from Lom through Leirdalen and the Høgvaglen pass, or through Visdalen and Urdadalen. And the animals were driven through the high passes at night, when the top layer of snow was frozen.

The grazing lands with their primitive drovers' huts, built from stone or plank, usually lay higher than the seters. Pastures privately owned were for hire; in that case it was the owner's duty to maintain a drovers' hut. And one drover might use several pastures, moving from one to another.

The grazing lands west of Bygdin were excellent, as were those in the Tyin region. Other good pastures were found in the area south of Bygdin and at that lake's northern shore. Heimdalen, Sikkilsdalen and Leirdalen were also used, as was Veodalen – here drovers still tend to their flocks. Several 19th century cattle traders are known by name; most of them came from Lom, Luster, Valdres and Årdal. Breikvam, west of Tyin, was Årdal land, and people from that community might have 3–400 heads of cattle and 40–50 horses grazing here. And the eastern shore of Tyin has alternately been used for Valdres seters and grazing lands.

The drovers generally were a tough breed, not spoiled by comforts. And they knew Stone Age man's trick of boiling food: if the kettle had been stolen from the drovers' hut, and that could happen, they made soup or porridge in wooden vessels by heating stones and throwing them in. But occasionally their cooking was more advanced. A well-known 19th century Norwegian author, A. O. Vinje, used to spend his summers at Eidsbu by Bygdin; close by a man from Luster, Kristian Heltne, tended to his drove. Heltne's living quarters were miserable, but he made excellent food, while Vinje had a good house and was a poor cook. So they made a deal: Heltne stayed in Vinje's house and cooked for the two of them. Heltne enjoyed his conversations with Vinje, and the discussions and arguments between the author and his friends, even more than he did having a decent roof above his head.

But as a rule the cattle men kept to their own rather rough company. And men from different communities exchanged yarns and local legends. Thus we know from Valdres a tale of violence originating in Lom, but forgotten in those parts: A few fellows had gone to a seter in the autumn to fetch home some hay. One of the men killed a hulder-child who kept tagging after him, bashing the kid's head against a wall. The silly fellow! he should have called for the kid's mother, and she surely would have fetched it. Now he was grabbed and violently thrown around, from one wall to another; he saw a furious woman attacking him, but the other men saw no one. And he was hurt so badly that he never regained his health.

At the end of August or in the beginning of September the drovers and their

In days of old the sheep were milked. But in later years those animals have pretty much been left to fend for themselves on the mountain pastures during summer. Gathering them in the autumn can be quite a task; many are the tales of people spending days searching for their sheep in rugged terrain. The picture below, of sheep being gathered in the month of October, is from Nausanosi seter, on the brink of Nosafjellet above Fortunsdalen. The mists in the background are rising, in the chilly autumn weather, from the lake by Skjolden and from Sognefjord.

Cattle trader from Gudbrandsdalen. The picture is from H. F. Hjorthøy's book describing the area AD 1785. The whips carried by those people were not uncommonly used as a means of self-defense; when returning from market bringing home a fair amount of money, the cattle traders were prone to attacks by robbers.

flocks left the mountains. Before leaving they gathered for a feast, usually at Nystøga on Fillefjell – and what mattered at that get-together, was being strongest and most agile. One year a fellow from [illegible] jumped so high that he not only kicked the rafter, but broke one of the ceiling boards. "That was a damned good feat!" said the owner of Nystøga. Whether he was of that opinion the following morning, is a different story.

Then came the driving of the animals to town, and there were special grazing grounds for them in the valley communities. But those droves must have been a sight to behold: The cattle trader led the way, on horseback or in a cart, after him came the drove of horses, then the huge flock of cattle, with herdsmen striving to keep them from straying. And the drovers were in no hurry, the animals were supposed to gain weight on the way. The traders were, however, proud men, not easily impressed. Once, in Gausdal, Per Flohaug, a big man from Luster, got angry when a gentleman in a carriage drawn by a team of two, forced his way from a side-road and into the middle of the drove. "That you have no right to do," said Per, grabbing both horses and holding them. The gentleman, belonging to a family of fame and influence, protested furiously and certainly did not conceal his identity. But Per did not budge, and that carriage stayed put until the entire drove had passed.

The return trip might be less glorious. It did happen that the traders sold each and every animal, including the horses, and *walked* home.

The railroad heralded the end of droving. Now the drovers' huts are falling down; a lot of people mistake them for hunters' huts – and most have probably been used by hunters too. And the drovers' trails may still be seen: deep ruts worn by many a hoof.

Industries of a Wilderness

Among the oldest industries of this country, is that of fashioning utensils from soapstone. Kettles were made from that material during the Viking Age – through subsequent centuries it has been used as building material, for tombstones, baptismal fonts, fireplaces, ovens –.

The old drovers' hut at Tvinnehaugen by Tyin (photo by K. Knudsen). The general description of such huts given by B. M. Keilhau in the year 1822 seems to fit rather well: "... huts, the inner part of which are dug into the ground, and which otherwise are built from rocks, pieces of sod and birch bark."

In Jotunheimen two old quarries, both in Lom, are known. One, actually a cluster of three, is found in Øvre Bøverdal, the other in Visdalen. Bits of tombstones, found under Lom's medieval church, prove that stone has been quarried in both places at least since the Middle Ages. And a number of legends exist about these quarries and about the men working there before they were given up in the 19th century. One rather flamboyant character was known as Tykkjestoren (The big man from Tykkje); he was a famed huntsman, a well-known carpenter and blacksmith and played the accordion, all this in addition to working the quarry.

Of the two quarries the one in Visdalen has been most thoroughly explored. It is found near the mouth of Grota, tributary to Visa; Grota springs from Grotbreene, the glaciers north of Glittertind's summit. The old Norse word "grjot" means stone; the river might have gotten its name because of the quarry, and the glaciers certainly got theirs from the river.

Soapstone was quarried here as long as usable material could be found, and several fireplaces in Lom reputedly have been built from Visdalen stone. A question unanswered was where that stone had been worked; we searched the area in the vicinity of the quarry, and found the overgrown foundations of a house. A trial excavation unearthed a thick layer of soapstone dust, refuse from production during a long period – we had located the workshop! Excavation of another site, further down the valley, proved that soapstone had been worked there during two different periods, the youngest layer of soapstone dust probably dating from the 18th or 19th century. But for how long has soapstone been quarried in Visdalen? Possibly since the Viking Age.

Except for the soapstone quarries and the bog iron production, Jotunheimen has not harboured much industrial activity. A few other quarries are found, for instance the one at Turtagrø, where flagstones for roofing have been taken. Then there have been charcoal kilns – some sawmills – production of tar and potash –. And there has been man's irrepressible dream of finding gold. But in Visdalen that hope is not entirely unrealistic; a few grains of gold may be found in the sands where Visa empties into Bøvra. However, the story of a man who found gold in Vettismorki, and never again was able to locate the spot, has all the earmarks of being a fairy tale.

Of Travelling, Trading and Going to the Fair

People of old preferred the mountain roads to those of the lowland; as a rule they were better, lying in open terrain, and steep hills were no obstacle to man or horse. Only the important ones had bridges and were maintained, but that went for the lowland roads too. Though "road" is too impressive a term for the pack trails that until some 150 years ago were the only overland means of communication in most parts of this country –.

Through Jotunheimen the main route running north-south was, and still is, the one across Valdresflya. The present road generally follows the old trail. However, the trail went south of Øvre and Nedre Sjodalsvatn, crossing Sjoa at the narrow canyon Ridderspranget, where that river has been bridged since medieval times.

Between east and west there were a southerly and a northerly route. And chance finds of a pair of spearheads from the Merovingian period, one in Kvikne (Fron), the other in the vicinity of Lærdal, points Fron out as the eastern terminus of an early southern trail; the spearheads, of eastern Norwegian type and practically identical, must have been forged in the same

workshop. This southern trail seems to have followed the n
Vinsteren, to have crossed Bygdin at Bygdissundet, then run
south of Bygdin towards Tyin, and finally to have branchec
trails: to Lærdal, to Årdal, to Luster – and going north to L
reasons unknown, names it the "Luster road" in Fron as we
The northern trail, more important in recent times, was on
dalen and Bøverdalen, and across Sognefjell to Fortun – a
eastern and western Norway now follows this route. In a cou
old trail did, however, climb higher than does the present
from Ottadalen at Garmo, as the main road also does, but
crosses a low ridge, going back into Ottadalen, the trail ke
cutting across through mountain valleys and passes, to Gløm
len. And where the main road takes off from Bøverdalen a
Leirdalen for a stretch, the trail climbed up on the ridge between those two valleys, and kept to that. Across Sognefjell there were several routes in addition to the one followed by the road; they were used at different times of the year, depending on the lay of snowdrifts and whether bogs and lakes were frozen. According to tradition there are 7 cairn-marked trails between Fortun and Lom. One, no longer well known, but previously much used, climbs up Slampeløyfte from Høydalen in Lom, goes across Storvatnet and Skålavatnet and descends steeply into Fortunsdalen at Løyfti. This is the shortest stretch across, and was used in early spring, for instance if people from Lom had to go to Sogn to buy seed grain after a year of poor crops. A group of 12–14 would-be emigrants, heading for the United States, were caught by a blizzard on that crossing about a 100 years ago and froze to death.

That mountain travelling involved a certain amount of risk was, however, taken for granted in those days. And people were wary of using the high trails

From the excavation of a seter site at Smiugjelsøygarden in Visdalen the summer of 1968. Two greyish layers of powdered soapstone, debris from a production of objects from that material, are visible; the bottom one might, just possibly, date back to the Middle Ages. The dark layers consist of decomposed organic matter.

View of Bøverdalen, looking north-east from the seter community of Mytingen by Galdhø.

in winter. But a blizzard could occur at any time of the year, even if very unlikely in summer. And quite a few have lost their lives on the trails of Jotunheimen. Some also have managed to save themselves in unusual ways – a man from Luster survived a blizzard on Sognefjell by killing his horse and seeking shelter inside the carcass –.

And from the Middle Ages we have laws regarding housing for travellers; those houses were called "sæluhus". The word is a combination of the old Norse "sál", meaning "soul", and the word for house; the implication is supposed to be that one could serve the salvation of one's soul by contributing to the erection and maintenance of such houses. I shall attempt to translate part of the old law while keeping some of its peculiarities of language – in its own way it gives an idea of the state of affairs: "In sæluhus all have equal rights . . . all shall be inside if there is room for all to be seated. If some have been there three nights unnecessarily, then they are next to leave; otherwise it shall be tossed for who has to leave. Then it is well if they leave who are supposed to according to the casting of lots. But if they will not, then they shall pay a fine to the King as for robbery, and they shall pay full fine (as for murder) for those who according to the casting of lots should have been inside, if they die outside." In or near Jotunheimen are three sites that, according to tradition or for other reasons, have been pointed out as possible locations of sæluhus. One is by Steinbusjøen (south of Bygdin and on the "Luster road" of legend); that one has been excavated and supposedly dates from early medieval times. Another is near Tyinholmen, and a third in Visdalen.

People of earlier ages rarely travelled just for the pleasure of it. But a journey could be undertaken with a number of purposes: bringing an important message, going to a wedding, looking after one's property –. And to people of Valdres and the Ottadalen region Bergen was, and has until fairly recently been, "the town" that people visited if they had errands to such a place; crossing the mountains to the western fjords and going from there by boat to Bergen, was faster and easier than to travel the cumbersome roads to Oslo. The main reasons for travelling were, however, pilgrimages and trade.

The only pilgrim road through Jotunheimen went from Bergen via Luster across Sognefjell to Lom, then on to Nidaros (Trondheim) and the famed shrine of St. Olav – though occasional groups of pilgrims may have travelled across Valdresflya on their way to the miraculous spring of St. Sunniva at Selja, an island off the western coast. And as the Lom church also is supposed to have had a reputation for miracles, some may have made a point of travelling that way and stopping there too. Those medieval flocks of pilgrims must have been a strange medley of people. One may imagine them, led by a priest who ever so often began to sing a hymn, the group joining in: people humbly doing penance, fingering their rosaries and muttering their Aves and Paternosters; people with the light of hope shining in their eyes, expecting an answer to fervent prayers – and a sprinkling of adventurers or outright scoundrels who took advantage of their travelling companions, even stole from them. King Erik Magnusson had his reasons when, in a royal letter of protection for pilgrims (issued towards the end of the 13th century), he distinguished between "true pilgrims" and fakers.

As for the trade, that was, as trade is prone to be, governed by people's need to buy and sell. People from Valdres and the Gudbrandsdalen region went to the fjord country of western Norway to buy salt and herring, and they offered

Pedalling along where people through millennia have walked the old trail across Valdresflya. In the far background Bitihorn, somewhat closer Synshorn, where a famous Valdresflya wanderer, Christen Smith, botanized in the year 1813.

"Kønnsteinn'", "the grain boulder", by the shore of Høydalsvatnet in Lom, on a route commonly used by men of that community when they had to travel to Sogn early in spring to buy seed grain. The grain was hauled across the mountains on sleds. But as the snow at that time of the year had melted in the valley, the men left them and their precious cargo in the shelter of Kønnsteinn' and went to fetch packhorses.

for sale furs, hides, bog iron and butter. Then there was a trading, both ways, of cattle and horses. The traffic does not seem to have been hampered by a law, existing from the Middle Ages until well into the 19th century, forbidding all trade outside of the towns – bartering being the sole exception –. And people of the Jotunheimen region kept gathering at their annual fairs; it would be unrealistic to imagine that only bartering took place at those.

Fairs were held, among other places, in Lom and Vågå. But most famous was the one by the church of St. Thomas in Smeddalen, on the mountain crossing between Valdres and Lærdal. People gathered there from the entire Jotunheimen region and from communities to the south and west. The Smeddalen fairs may even predate Christianity, officially introduced into Norway in the 11th century; some historians suggest an origin in pagan cults with ritual combat between men from the various communities, horseracing and horsefights. And it is certain that combat as well as horseracing have been features of the St. Thomas' fairs of later years; a saying goes that at those "many a horse was disabled, and many a powerful man was beaten up". According to a local tradition people of early medieval times lived year-round in Smeddalen, then a centre of bog iron production – which might explain the presence of a church in what is now a seter region.

However, the medieval history of the church as well as of the fair is lost in a haze of legends; written records do not appear until the 17th century. Then a pastor of Vang in Valdres, the parish to which St. Thomas' was appended, had the church repaired, and resumed annual services in connection with the fairs – at that time services had been discontinued for an uspecified number of years, possibly since the reformation (Lutheranism became the official faith of Norway by royal decree in the year 1537). And strangely for that post-reformation period, St. Thomas' seems immediately to have gained, or maybe it never had lost, a reputation for miracles. Pilgrims flocked to the church, donating gifts in the hope of reaping divine favors. This ado, in addition to the fair's reputation of brawls and loose morals, caused so much of a scandal that a suggestion of razing the church was put forward in the 1740's. Luck alone saved it: it was warmly defended by a Danish pastor who had ended up in Vang by mistake, thinking he had been assigned another parish by the same name, and who remained there for one year only. But in the year 1808

Overleaf: Autumn in the mountains.

indignation had reached such proportions that the church of St. Thomas was doomed; it was levelled to the ground in August of that year.

Thus, sadly, ended the only enterprise combining the old occasions for travelling the Jotunheimen trails: pilgrimage and trade.

Tales of Robbers and Outlaws

Law and order seem to have been kept fairly well in this country during the Middle Ages, and travelling the mountain trails to have been pretty safe. One reason why travellers went unmolested may, however, have had nothing to do with law-abidingness, namely the fact that they tended to move about in large groups – a phenomenon that has been explained as a symptom of a prevailing group mentality. According to this same theory the individualism that became part of the Renaissance way of thinking, also found expression in people's travelling habits; a new tendency to travel alone or in small groups is seen as the cause of an increase in assault and robbery during the 16th century. Later King Christian V's law of the year 1687 is blamed when the state of affairs takes a turn for the even worse at about that time. Earlier Norwegian laws had stuck to the ancient Norse system of fines, under which manslaughter did not necessarily carry a death penalty. A fellow who had, as the saying went, "had the bad luck of killing a man" – strong beer and hard liquor ran freely and tempers ran hot, and a minor quarrel could turn into a tragedy –, was able to make amends and remain a free man, even if the fine reduced him to poverty. The new law changed that, enforcing the principle that a life had to be given in payment for a life taken. This meant that any man who "had the bad luck etc." automatically became an outlaw, unless caught, and that, since he had already forfeited his life, only his own conscience would eventually keep him from killing again.

All this theorizing may, up to a point, be relevant to the actual situation, which might have been more complex. As to Jotunheimen, it is true that tales of assault and robbery abound from the period of the late 1600's and on. But outlaws, in the sense described above, do not dominate the picture. That honour goes to bands of tramps who were travelling about, terrorizing people in general. And surprisingly often local people, and not necessarily the poor, seem to have supplemented their incomes with a bit of robbery.

According to tradition that was the case on the mountain crossing between Valdres and Lærdal during one period. About a century ago a drover, Gudbrand Thune, swore that he had met the ghost of a man named Heggland by Tyin; Heggland had been murdered there a good many years before that. And the ghost story angle underscores the fact that these tales are legends, more or less reliable, more or less embroidered upon as they have been retold time and again. Still, they probably give a fairly good idea of the dangers of travelling in those days, especially if carrying any amount of money. Cattle traders returning from town, peddlers who had sold their wares, people on their way home after having made a good deal of any sort, were often kept track of. And they did wisely to find trustworthy travel companions when setting out across the mountains, or at least to be well armed. Sognefjell, frequently travelled, seems to have been a favorite haunt of robbers; many a man is said to have been killed and robbed there, and then buried to conceal the crime.

But some got away to tell about it.

One such story concerns a man from Lom, Nils Bakkeberg. He was returning from Luster on horseback, carrying a great deal of money – and a loaded gun. Suddenly, as he was approaching the highest point of the trail, a big, threatening man appeared as if out of nowhere, and came at him. Nils, suspecting that the fellow had lain in ambush, took aim with his gun: "Don't come too close!" But the man kept heading for him. "If you come any closer, I shoot!" Nils warned; the fellow was within range. "That gun is not loaded, brother," was the reply, and the big man kept on coming. "You shall find out," said Nils. "One more step, now, and I fire!" The man was so near that he could almost reach the gun barrel when Nils pulled the trigger, the roar of the gun splitting the air. The man dropped to the ground, dead, and Nils did not tarry about reloading his weapon. Then he noticed that the dead man was wearing a large silver brooch; he jumped off his horse and grabbed it. But he did not bother to see if the fellow was carrying more stolen goods. And as he rode on, he turned and saw a whole gang of tramps peeking out from behind a boulder – evidently none felt like pursuing him. However, the following year, when Nils was at the fair in Lærdal, a man he did not know came up to him, remarking: "You are a good shot!" "Aw – only fair," said Nils. "Yes, you are, and you killed quite a buck at Sognefjell last year, but you didn't take the trouble of skinning him. And that was good for you – if you had tried, *you* would have lost your hide."

Another man, named Gunnar, also setting out alone with quite a bit of money, cunningly dressed in the worst rags he could get his hands on. And sure enough, he ran into a band of tramps; they threatened to kill him if he did not hand over whatever money or valuables he might carry. "You won't get rich from that,", said Gunnar, "but I shall gladly give you all of my four skillings." (about four pence). The tramps, looking at his rags, believed him and let him go; they did not even take his four skillings!

While the tramps of these stories are anonymous and seem identical, the local bandits have names and personalities. A couple of those, known as the Sperstad-rascals, both owned farms in Ottadalen and were well off; nevertheless they were a scourge to travellers on the mountain trails during the first half of the 18th century. And their crimes certainly were not haphazard. Once they had been keeping track of a peddler, a fellow named Jo, who came from the western fjord country; he had sold most of his wares and ought to be heading for home soon. And when Jo set out from Lom, so late in autumn that people had left the seters, they had figured how far he would go before he settled down for the night. The place they had in mind was Bøverkinnhalsen, between Leirdalen and Bøverdalen. And there, by his campfire, they found Jo. They went at him, and even though Jo put up quite a fight, they finally managed to beat him unconscious with a rock, grabbed his money and left – one of them returned a little later to make sure that he was really dead, and when he was not, finished him off. This story became known because the villains spent the night in a barn, chatting amiably about their misdeed, and not knowing that another fellow also had found shelter there. That man was, however, too frightened to take his story to the authorities. And the peddler's corpse was not found until next spring. The Sperstad-rascals were never punished for their crimes – though one of them is said to have committed suicide.

But among the most colorful of these tales is the one about "Øyrlous-Kari" ("Earless-Kari") and her sons:

Kari was a widow and her home a tenant farm high on the slope above Glømsdal in Bøverdalen. She had three sons. And the boys were eager at

learning all kinds of sports, especially knife-throwing and gunplay; people were horrorstricken when Kari turned up one day with both her ears missing. "The little fellows have had some fun," said Kari. The three soon were able to beat any kid in the community at any game. And once, when Kari saw them win, she blurted out: "Those geldings of mine do best anyway!" Thus people found out what she had done to the boys, and gathered that cutting her ears off had been their revenge. When the three grew up, they took to robbery and murder like ducks to the water. And they became a terror on the mountain crossing between Vårdalen and Glømsdal, lying in ambush for travellers. Soon the three of them, Eivind, Segert and Hendrik, were more than well off – which did not make them retire from crime. Hendrik even found himself new hunting grounds at Sognefjell and did very well there. But after a while the good people of Lom and Luster had had more than enough of him. Men from both communities joined and hunted him down. And when they had caught him, they didn't bother about details of legal procedure; they drove an iron hook into a cliff and hung him from that. Segert lasted a while longer; he was caught a couple of times, but managed to escape. But he, too, got his desert, and in his case after due trial and judgement. He was executed by sword in Lom, and a lot of people turned out to watch the fun. But Segert had a trick up his sleeve yet. He asked permission to say a few last words, and when that was granted, stated that he had a large kettle full of silver hidden under a bridge in Vårdalen – that man could have it who got there first! There was a great commotion, people ran to their horses and set out on a mad ride towards Vårdalen, some almost disabling their mounts. But, unfortunately for Segert, enough stayed put to see to it that his head was duly severed from his body. The kettle, however, was found where Segert had told people to look. Eivind, the third brother, did better. He moved on to another community, there to become – schoolmaster!

The legends about "regular" outlaws, who might have committed some crime in a fit of temper, and lived in the woods or mountain areas to avoid the arm of the law, seem to indicate that at least some of those tried to make an honest living. And it seems that people gave them a helping hand, much more so than they were supposed to according to the letter of the law.

One such outlaw turned up in Øystre Slidre (Valdres) some 250 years ago.

Left: Dream of the cloudberry fancier – and which Norwegian isn't one? Though also growing in the lowlands, those little delicacies (actual size some 1½ cm diameter) are considered mainly "fruits of the mountains".
Right: "No frog's leg fanciers here in Jotunheimen – I hope – ?"

People soon realized that this was a man of great learning, and after a while pried out that he was a clergyman who had killed somebody. But he never told his name. He settled in Kalvedalen near Bitihorn, and became known as "Kalvedalspresten", "the Kalvedal minister". But he spent much of his time at Lykkja, a nearby farm, where he became friends with Hallvard, a huntsman and the farmer's younger brother. Hallvard in Lykkja learned so much from Kalvdalspresten that he, too, became famed for his learnedness.

But are any traces to be found of such outlaws in Jotunheimen today?

Maybe. Occasionally people happen upon caves that seem to have been someone's home – implements are found that do not belong in a hunter's lair. In Lom I have heard of two such caves, one in the Sognefjell region, the other in Heimfjellet above Garmo. But if outlaws have used those, there is one thing only to be said: they lived miserable lives.

The Falcon Trappers

The earliest proof that falconry (hawking) was known in Norway, is a picture carved on a stone (first half of the 11th century), showing a rider on horseback with a bird sitting on his arm. And Norwegian laws of that period or somewhat later mention the catching of hawks, establishing the landowner's exclusive right to catch such birds on his land. However, when the regional codes of law were replaced by "landsloven" ("the law of the country") in the year 1276, a clause was added giving the king an option of buying the birds and a right to catch them wherever he might please. That clause was repeated in the laws of king Christian IV (1604) and king Christian V (1687).

Norwegian and Icelandic falcons were considered among the best, and during the Middle Ages the town of Bergen became a falcon trading centre. The price of a trained bird was prohibitingly high. And falconry was truly a sport of kings and noblemen – while the peregrine falcon, which catches its prey while on the wing, was considered the noblest of hawks. A hunt followed this general pattern: The falconer sets out on horseback with the bird sitting on his arm, protected by a heavy leather glove. When a suitable quarry is observed, he throws the falcon into the air, and the chase begins. The falcon rises above the prey while pursuing it, the falconer follows the direction of the hunt. Then comes the moment when the falcon dives for the quarry and brings it down. Now the huntsman rides as fast as possible to get to the big bird before it devours its catch. Then he calls it back to his arm.

The simplest way to catch hawks, including falcons, was to rob their nests of eggs or chicks, the procedure indicated by early Norwegian laws. Those birds did, however, never attain the hunting skills of birds raised in freedom. But not until the 14th century is trapping of mature hawks mentioned in this country. A couple of centuries later foreigners began to trap the big birds in Norway – and from that period on the kings gradually usurped the trapping rights, making those a royal prerogative; during the latter part of the 16th and the 17th century they even leased the rights to trappers from Brabant, who were considered Europe's best.

By then hawk trapping had developed into a rather complex operation, the trick being to catch the birds entirely undamaged. In Norway the trapping took place in late summer, and huts constructed for the purpose were used. They were circular, partly dug in the ground, and with a view in all directions. A whole array of equipment was employed: a cage containing a shrike, this was put on the roof or close by; several tall poles erected near the hut –

through holes at the top of those ran lines which could be manipulated from the hut; a live pidgeon tied to one of those lines and a trained hawk to another – the latter was supposed to make an approaching wild bird feel secure, an artificial or stuffed bird could also serve this purpose –, in addition there might be a display of various decoys, including bundles of feather; finally, bow nets, camouflaged on the ground and equipped with lines (to be maneuvered from the hut). Now, when the shrike gave warning that a bird of prey was in the vicinity, a whole little play was performed: the fluttering pidgeon was pulled up and down, the trained hawk and the various equipment set in motion. And at the very moment when the wild hawk dug its claws into the poor pidgeon, both were pulled down in front of the nets, which were then thrown over them, entrapping both.

During the 18th century the demand for trained falcons decreased; by the year 1800 trapping had just about ceased in Norway. But in the Jotunheimen region a couple of sites of trappers' huts still are known: remnants of a stone wall encircles a depression in the ground, surrounded by heaps of rocks, which have been used to secure the poles – nearby may also be found the site of the cabin where the trappers lived. In Skåbu, not far from Nedre Heimdalsvatn and on a mountain named "Falkfengerfjelle" ("Falcon trapper mountain"), one such site was located in the year 1972; one of the poles was found practically intact. Another site, well documented by local tradition, but not yet located, is on Skarvhøn some 5 km east of Lemonsjøen. And it appears that people of the area looked with great distrust upon those foreign trappers – even suspecting them of witchcraft because they consistently kept visitors out of their cabin. But the reason for this seeming secretiveness probably was the necessity of protecting newly trapped birds from whatever might frighten them.

In later years foreign hawk catchers have returned to Norway – the sport of falconry is gaining in popularity. Those people, pretending to be ornitologists, but really out to rob the nests of eggs or chicks, are *not* welcome. The big hawks, the Falco peregrinus and the Falco rusticolus, are protected by law in this country, and are on the list of endangered species.

Råkåvatnet (north of Ottadalen) is one of the locations in the Jotunheimen vicinity where falcon trappers practiced their art. The rough stone hut in the picture is hardly the original one, but more likely a shelter built from the ruins of the falcon trappers' lair.

Way-out Farming

According to one theory people lived year-round in the mountains during late Iron Age, maybe even after that. Finds in Jotunheimen and nearby areas have neither proven nor disproven this. But legends of abandoned mountain farms and communities exist, for instance the one of Smeddalen, and they are usually related to the Black Death. Visdalen is also supposed to have been settled – which is entirely possible, a combination of cattle farming, hunting, bog iron production and soapstone quarrying could have provided a fairly decent living for a small community.

From modern times a number of rather inaccessible farms in the vicinity of settled areas are known, examples being Fuglesteg and Furås in Fortun, and the now abandoned Avdal in Årdal. However, farms in the actual wilderness, far from the habitats of other men, have been rare. A family lived in Sikkilsdalen a number of years during the 19th century; before tourism, their sources of income were cattle farming and hunting/trapping – bears, for instance, were plentiful in the area. But best known are the farms of Utladalen, Vetti and Vormeli. And that valley is different from every other in Jotunheimen: a wild, deep canyon cutting into the most rugged mountain area – one has to travel far before the canyon floor reaches an altitude of 600 m.

Vetti is located at a little above 300 m, where the canyon seems to widen grudgingly, giving room for some acres of farmland. According to tradition people lived there before the Black Death; a migratory legend has even become associated with the place: "Once upon a time", when each region of Norway had its own king, a king, famed for his strength, lived at Vetti. He fell in love with Ingeborg, beautiful daughter of the king at Ornes in Luster, and went to Ornes to ask for her hand in marriage. But the Ornes king deceitfully made him a prisoner, tying him with a rope made from Ingeborg's silken hair, and that the Vetti king could not make himself tear asunder. So he was killed. And the desolate Ingeborg drowned herself in a lake in the mountain region between Årdal and Luster – it is still named after her.

However that may be, a written record of Vetti does not exist until the year 1600, when the farm is registered as abandoned. And the first man known to have lived at Vetti was named Erik; he came there as a tenant

Deserted farm. Avdal, a couple of kilometers from neighbouring farms in Årdal, is sitting on the brink of Vettisgjelet, and access to the place has been extremely difficult. The British mountaineer Wm. C. Slingsby visited Avdal in the year 1875 and thus describes the path (later replaced by a somewhat more serviceable one) connecting that farm with the rest of the world: "(it) is the very acme of perfection of a romantic mountain path, and a model of rustic engineering. ...The house stands on the brink of a grand cataract, the Afdalsfos, and close to the top f this fall is a wild "devil's bridge" over the glacial stream. In some places the path is excavated in the face of an overhanging rock, in others, instead of excavating, wooden bridges span dizzy precipices and connect different spurs of rock. Where feasible, the track is built up from terraces below. Except at the top, the waterfall is not visible from the path, but its spray is carried over it by the wind, and keeps fresh the many plants of Saxifraga cotyledon whose lovely white sprays gladden the eyes of all who behold them." For more than 300 years people lived at Avdal, winter and summer – .

Hauling firewood by packhorse is an old tradition in Jotunheimen. Wood was scarce near some of the seters, and much was needed to keep the fires going under the big kettles used for cheese-making. Occasionally seters had to be abononed for lack of firewood, and the menfolk commonly brought a load when they came up weekends with a horse to fetch the produce. This picture was taken in the vicinity of Skogadalsbøen.

farmer in the year 1603. The access to the place, through the Vetti gorge, was difficult and dangerous, yet people have lived there ever since. The first owner-farmer was Jørgen Arnfinnsson, who bought the place in the year 1775; his descendants still live at Vetti, now hosting the tourist lodge. Eventually land was cleared for at least three tenant farms, in addition to the main farmstead. And hunting and trapping were parts of the way of life. But even if the location is rugged – the main farm has had to be moved because of a danger of landslides – people kept their sense of humor. Of Ola, a 19th century tenant farmer, the saying in the community went that he was an exceptionally amenable man. Because if Ola offered a guest a drink of liquor, and the guest politely objected that "This is much too kind of you!" – then he retorted: "Right you are!" and promptly corked the bottle.

But Vetti is no longer isolated from the rest of the world; a tractor road running through the Vetti gorge, a community project undertaken by the people of Årdal, was completed this year.

The other Utladalen farm, Vormeli, lies at an altitude of some 600 m, where Maradalen comes plunging down from Skagastølstindene. Here, too, the gorge widens a bit; the place is known as Utladalshole, "the Utladal hollow". A legend has it that the first man to settle came around the year 1600, in which case he must have made his living from hunting and trapping. Farmland was not cleared there until the 1780's, when two men from Fortun were awarded a land-improvement prize for that feat. One of them settled at Vormeli and stayed some 20 years. The soil of the "hollow" is excellent; grain and potatoes give good crops, and several families made Vormeli their home in the 18th and 19th centuries. However, the loneliness of the place was extreme; a visit to the nearest neighbours at Vetti was a matter of a 4–5 hour strenuous hike each way. And the distance to the parish church in Fortun was more than 30 km, involving a climb of 900 m to the Keisaren pass between Skagastølstindene and Fanaråken, and a descent of 1490 m from there to Fortun. A special house at Vormeli was used if any one died during the winter; the dead was left there until spring, when it became possible to bring him or her to the cemetery. And in the year 1867 the last man to farm Vormeli collected his earthly goods and his herd of goats and left for Årdal, where he sold the animals and moved back to Fortun.

But the home in the "hollow" may not have been quite as awful a place as it seems according to a visitor's description of the year 1859: "A wretched one-room cottage, smoke-filled, with a floor of stone slabs and sinister, darkened walls, is the living quarters of the people who here, in a kind of exile, live a miserable life." The mountaineer Emanuel Mohn, who visited Vormeli in the 1870's, goes into raptures describing the "lush, sun-drenched birchwoods" and "the deep, cold, greenish-white waters of the Utla". And according to a general description of the area, made in the 1890's, the farmers of Vormeli had "made a good living, having a sizable income from hunting".

The bear hunting, anyhow, was exceptionally good in Utladalen. And many a legend concerns the running battle between the bruins and the Vormeli farmers. One man supposedly got so hopping mad when a bear had killed his best goat, that he hit the beast with what he happened to have at hand, which was a sack full of fodder – after the ensuing struggle the man's clothes had to be cut loose from his arms.

During a period Vormeli was used as a seter; after that it lay abandoned for years. But recently one of the seter houses has been restored, the project being supported by the Norwegian Tourist Association.

A Thousand Years of Quarrelling – and a Little Bit about Peace

Grazing rights have been a main issue of squabbles and enmity between people within the various Jotunheimen communities – especially during the 18th and 19th centuries when seter farming as well as droving hit their peaks. There have also been quarrels and legal battles over fishing rights.

Between communities the struggle has focused on the establishment of regional borders in the mountain area, a struggle that has been violent, and has produced a number of legal battles and much paper-work.

People of Valdres and Vågå have fought over hunting rights in the Gjende-Valdresflya region and over hunting and fishing rights to Nedre Heimdalen – 6 parchments dating from the period 1336–1628 were needed to establish that the farm Sandbu in Vågå had been given rights to that valley by king Sverre (1150–1202). And the quarrel is not yet forgotten; the big, official "Bygdebok for Valdres" ("Book of the Valdres Communities") states, in the year 1964, that "that was an unlawful act committed by king Sverre". Between men from Valdres and Fron the "bone of contention" has been the fishing rights in Vinsteren and Sandvatnet. A document of the year 1558 states that an agreement has been reaced upon "many years of discord, hatred, envy and strife". But that agreement, if sincere, certainly did not endure – and as late as in the year 1815 a regular fight, involving a number of men from each community, took place on the ice of Sandvatnet. Between

Årdal and Luster the upper part of Utladalen has been a disputed territory. Between people from Lom and Vågå fishing rights in Rindtjønn by Tesse and hunting rights in Veodalen have been matters of conflict. Even the men from Lom and Valdres, of whom one should think that miles of rugged mountain terrain ought to keep them safely apart, have got into brawls over hunting rights. The communities of Vang in Valdres and Årdal have had an ancient quarrel running regarding fishing and hunting at Breikvam, west of Tyin; the finale was a court battle concerning fishing rights in Breikvam's brooks and rivers, the decision being handed down in the year 1915. And the fighting spirit lives on – people of Lom and Luster presently have a legal battle going regarding hunting rights and ownership of reindeer on Sognefjell. But it would be unjust to look at all this as a matter of orneriness. To people of an earlier age, and one does not have to go back very far, starvation was a real threat; those hunting and fishing rights might be a matter of life and death.

However, a millenium (or more) of quarrels and fights has left a rich heritage of legends – naturally the local boys everywhere are given the honour of having beaten up everybody else. But one legend of this type, from Øystre Slidre, Valdres, has an unusual twist: Two brothers, Hallvard in Lykkja ("Kalvedalspresten»s friend) and Big-Ola got into a quarrel on Valdresflya with a Vågå man called "Klæppin" (this seems to have been "Strong-Tjøstol" Kleppe, of hunting and fighting fame). Ola and Klæppin got into a fight, and Ola did so well that Hallvard was worried he should kill the other fellow. He

This parchment, of the year 1336, affirms the claim that Ivar Gjesling, owner of the farm Sandbu in Vågå, had been given rights to Heimdalsvatnet by King Sverre (1151-1202).

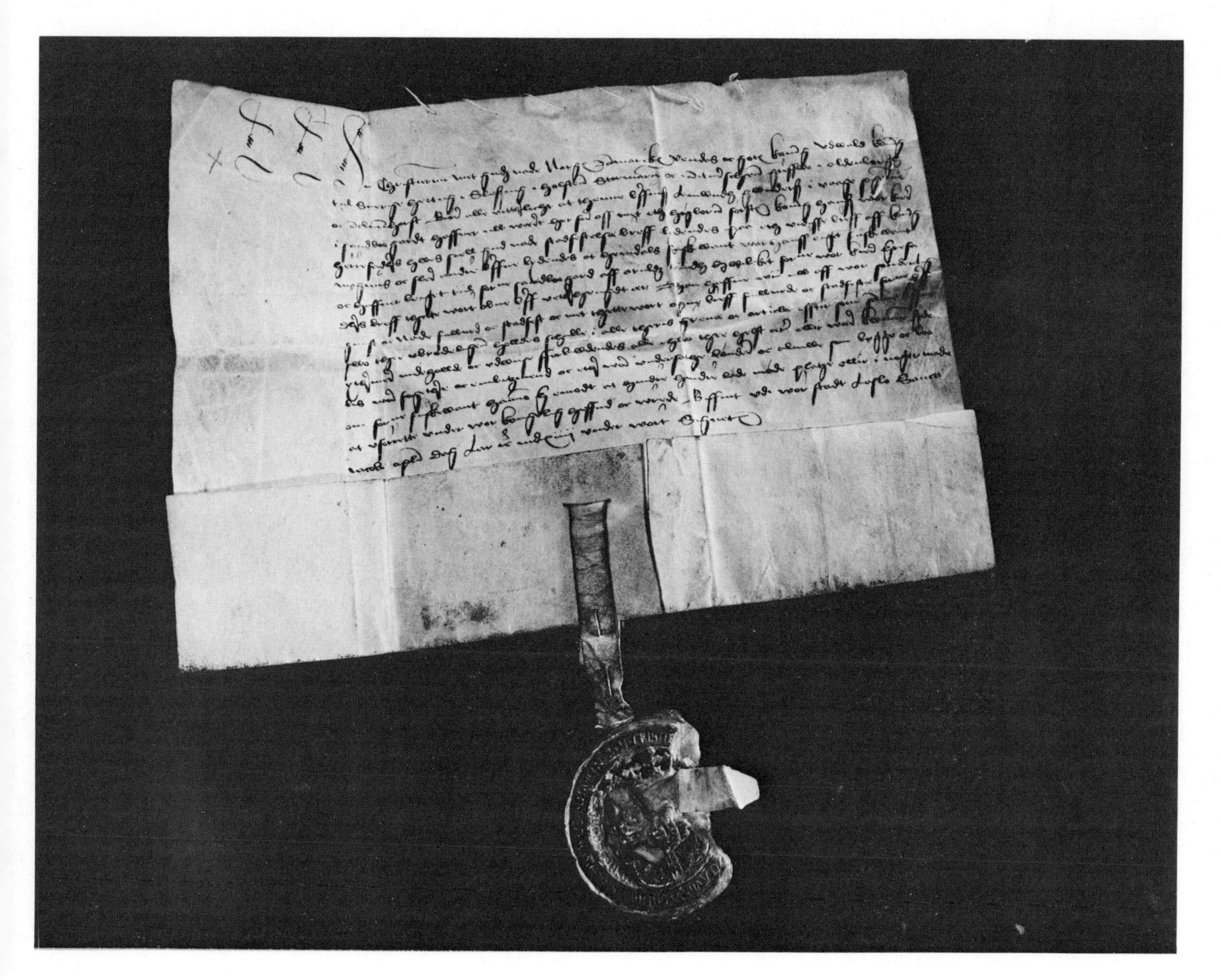

ran for cover and screamed for help at the top of his voice. Ola, thinking Hallvard was being attacked, let go of Klæppin and rushed to rescue his brother. He got furious at having been fooled – Hallvard headed for Lykkja, running as fast as he could, with Ola in hot pursuit. But Ola shortly calmed down, and Hallvard then said: "You ought to thank God, now, that you were saved from becoming an outlaw!"

But above and beyond local squabbles and fights has been a struggle, through the centuries, between the crown and the local communities for ownership of Jotunheimen's vast areas of mountain "commons". According to the sagas some sort of royal claim to lordship of all the land was put forth around the year 900; the context and meaning of this is, however, unclear. And not until some 300 years later does the crown clearly claim ownership to the mountain commons. Another 400 years passed before the term "the King's commons" was used for the first time (in king Christian IV's law of the year 1604). Since that time the controversy mainly has concerned what part of the area was to be considered as "the King's commons". The final decision was not made until a commisson, making its enquiries during the 1920's and -30's, decided the matter mainly to the advantage of the government. But one of Jotunheimen's townships, Vang in Valdres, flatly refused to yield. When an earlier commission had treated the same matter in the year 1757, the spokesman of the Vang farmers insisted that "Here in Vang is no 'King's commons', only a 'commons' belonging to farmers". Now the people of Vang took their case all the way to Supreme Court, and won in a decision of the year 1951.

Late autumn – the mountains are resting in a gentle silence; ice, bluish-white, is crusting along riverbanks with yellow grass and brown leaves; dark rocks burden sloping mountainsides rising towards the snow of approaching winter.

Gentle silence and a blessed peace. Man's struggles through a thousand years, the struggles and conflicts one carries within oneself – all seem to dissolve in this peace, like a handful of salt thrown into a lake. Then all boundaries, all distances of time and space disappear – one is in unity with all the world, with men and women everywhere, past and present, a unity of suffering and happiness, of struggle and rest.

But then – a bothersome uneasiness.

This peace, breaking the limits of the ego, giving birth to true compassion, is not unchangeable. It is defenseless and easily damaged. We, the people of our century, have the skills, the means, to alter these mountains, to leave them indelibly marked by our greed.

Do we also have the wisdom to leave them alone?

Autumn in Jotunheimen. By Tyin.

A Wilderness "Discovered"

Vera Henriksen

Enter: the Explorers

The skald of the old Norse mythological poem "Voluspá" ("Prediction of the sorceress", probably dating from the second half of the 10th century) describes a new earth, appearing after the cataclysmic destruction of our present version in a violent struggle involving powers, good and evil:

> Up she sees rising
> a second time
> earth from the seas,
> once again green.
>
> Above the waterfalls
> soars the eagle,
> bird that catches
> fish in the mountains.

And an appreciation of nature and its vistas seems to be innate in man, the artist. A Norwegian archeologist, specializing in the Stone Age, once told me that beauty of scenery could be a deciding factor for Stone Age man when picking a place to sit down to make himself some implement – tell-tale chips of flint give him away. But fashion, originating in trend-setting circles and changing through the centuries, as a rule has dictated to the pliable majority what kind of scenery they ought to consider beautiful.

Thus in historic times, which in Norway means the last millennium, the assessment of a wilderness like Jotunheimen's jumble of peaks, glaciers and waterfalls has been subject to prevailing European trends within philosophy and art. Which means that for centuries the mountains aroused no particular interest; they were there by act of God – known and taken for granted by the people of the area, looked upon as a wasteland from the point of view of agriculture and considered a trial to be suffered by travellers who had to cross them. At the beginning of the 17th century a topographical work mentions that "west of Gudbrandsdalen are situated terrible, high mountains and peaks". A century and a half later a writer on the same subject does not even mention the existence of high mountains in the area, and a map published in the year 1785 indicates mountains of moderate height.

However, by that time the Age of Enlightenment had dawned on Europe, even on these northern shores. One result was a number of topographical works on the country's various provinces, this being further encouraged in the 1780's by a prize offered in the name of His Royal Highness Prince Frederik. In an early (pre-competition) essay, the author, a Valdres clergyman, notes that a "mountain above the mountains" exists between Valdres and Gudbrandsdalen. And that good man, having heard of the old trail across Valdresflya, shudderingly comments about this relatively safe and comfortable

Next page: "West of Gudbrandsdalen are situated terrible, high mountains." Knutsholstind (2340 m) is highest among the peaks in the rugged region between Bygdin and Gjende.

Christen Smith, who went into an unknown region to botanize – and found Northern Europe's highest mountains.

mountain crossing that "God help the wanderer who there is caught in a blizzard or a fog; if he escapes with his life, he ought to look upon this as a special Grace from Our Lord." In the most famous such description of the area, one produced by a Gudbrandsdalen pastor in connection with the competition and published in the year 1885, the same high mountain between Fron and Valdres is named, the author adding: "There are also numerous other peaks that I shall not mention, as they are of no particular interest."

Thus the 18th century came to a close, as did the first two decades of the 19th, while those Norwegians who considered themselves enlightened, were totally unaware that the highest mountains of Northern Europe were situated in a terra incognita of Southern Norway, – within easy reach from Sognefjorden as well as from the country's main overland thoroughfares. Yet the Age of Enlightenment brought in its train Jotunheimen's "discovery".

The Pioneers

The world-famous Swedish botanist Carl von Linné (1707–78) had kindled a general interest in botany in Scandinavia. And Martin Vahl, a Danish botanist teaching at the university of Copenhagen, at that time the only such institution in the united kingdom Denmark-Norway, crossed Sognefjell in the year 1787. He was botanizing, and in the passing noted that this maybe was "the roughest mountain area of Norway". But his expedition caused hardly a ripple beyond the confines of a narrow circle of specialists.

However, among Vahl's pupils was a young Norwegian named Christen Smith – a student of medicine who, though graduating in that discipline in the year 1808, found his love and life work in botany. In the years 1812 and -13 he applied for and was given grants for extensive botanizing excursions in Norwegian mountain areas. It was in keeping with the times that there were strings attached: in addition to botanizing, establishing altitudes and making observations concerning geology, he was expected to be on the outlook for "potential sources of income for farmers, such as grazing land for goats and areas suitable for the culture of bees". Christen Smith came to the as yet un-named Jotunheimen in the year 1813. He climbed Bitihorn (south-east of Bygdin), broke his barometer while descending from that peak and thus was prevented from establishing any more altitudes, but undaunted continued to the northern shore of Bygdin. He botanized on Synshorn and Kalvåhøgda, then proceeded across Valdresflya to the eastern end of Gjende – where he also tended to his task of investigating potential sources of income by going reindeer hunting with local huntsmen. In addition he climbed Besshø, from which he could ascertain that the mountain massif included the highest peaks of Southern Norway. The following year he was named professor of botany at the fledgling Norwegian university in Oslo (founded in the year 1811). For reasons unknown he never wrote extensively on his Jotunheimen expedition, though voicing his enthusiasm for the alpine flora of the area. Two years later he took part in a British expedition to Zaire (then Congo), where he died, probably from a tropical disease.

Yet Christen Smith's enthusiasm had inspired another medical student with an inclination towards botany: Christian Peter Bianco Boeck. After exploring the Jotunheimen area from Valdres in the years 1818 and -19, he secured the company of Baltazar Mathias Keilhau, a fellow student at the Oslo university and a future professor of geology. In the summer of the year 1820 those two set out on the expedition that has later been labelled "Jotunheimen's disco-

The painter Johannes Flintoe's rendering of a sketch by B. M. Keilhau. Keilhau's description of the scene: "From a lesser peak in Koldedalen one has the most splendid view of Hurrungane's close formation with countless snow-fields and glaciers. Deep, narrow valleys run towards Sognefjord; the ice-water of small lakes and rivers are of a most lovely green hue. Morka-Koldedalen comes from Årdal up to this point, and Utladalen cuts far in between the peaks."

very". Accompanied by a local guide, the huntsman Ola Urden, they ascended Bitihorn and from there proceeded to the northern shore of Bygdin – as Smith had done before them. They climbed Kalvåhøgda, then followed the drovers' trail westward along the shore to Langedalen, up that valley, north of Galdeberg's summit and down to Bygdin near the western end of that lake. They continued across Eidet to Tyin, whereupon they made the first ascent of Falketind, at that time known as Morka-Koldedalstind. They did not, however, traverse the mountain area. Instead they went to Årdal, and on to Fortun by way of Fardalen. From Turtagrø they then climbed the northernmost peak of the Hurrungane massif, the easily accessible Nordre Skagastølstind, – whereafter they went on to other exploits further west.

The first of Keilhau's sensational reports on their sojourn in the rugged world of what he called "Jotunfjeldene" was published on September 21st of the year 1820 in a periodical named "Budstikken" (which may be roughly translated "The Messenger"). This was, however, not Budstikken's first article of the year mentioning that mountain area. The July and August issues had carried a topographical report on the Lærdal-Årdal region by Ulrik Bøyesen, pastor of the parish encompassing both of those valleys. Parts of that topographical article, with commentaries by the author, had even been published the year before in the weekly "Den norske Tilskuer" ("The Norwegian Observer"); I quote: "Hurrungane is a mountain massif in the parish of Luster ... going as far as to Utladalen. It contains many strange and spectacular peaks, and certainly the highest mountains in the diocese of Bergen. ... The mountains are surrounded by glaciers, while the peaks, black and horrifying, tower into the region of clouds." Bøyesen also gives the interesting piece of information that local people, when travelling between Årdal and Luster across the glaciers of one of the passes, made use of a rope "so that one man keeps walking ahead of another, keeping a certain distance, and if one falls into a crevasse, then the rest are not only warned, but are also able to pull him out." And that was more than 30 years prior to the "birth" of modern mountaineering in the Alps during the mid-1800's –.

Why, then, did Bøyesen's article go practically unnoticed, while Keilhau's

Falketind to the right, Hjelledalstind to the left. But the lake in the foreground, Koldedalsvatnet, is hardly Keilhau's "tiny lake". A little further west, between the two peaks, is a tarn that fits his description better.

Keilhau's rendering of Kalvåhøgda and the view north.

caused a sensation? The Age of Romanticism was upon the land, and Bøyesen's fairly dry topographical notes did not strike people's fancy. Keilhau, on the other hand, was a man of his time, with a keen sense of the dramatic as well as the flamboyant; he was also an able author. Here is his description of the view north from Kalvåhøgda: "Horrible precipices encircle a dreadful valley, on all sides surrounded by glacier cataracts, while a glacier covers the valley floor. Snowdrifts protrude like roofs from the top of steep walls, when tumbling, they cause turbulent avalanches –." Of Koldedalen: "The peaks thrust their black spires towards frightening heights. . . . The valley is, however, surrounded by less towering mountains carrying eternal snow on their backs, while dreadful-beautiful glaciers run down their dark-green sides, . . . the tremendous, rigid bodies of ice seem to move, now advancing, now retreating. The valley is dominated by huge heaps of rocks, grey and yellow moss being the only vegetation. A tiny lake, still dotted with ice floes at the end of July, fills part of the valley basin. . . . the cold lake with its dead, grey-and-yellow shores, the chaos of boulders, the bluish-green, weirdly shaped glaciers, the fields of snow pierced by threatening alpine forms, make a strong impression, heightened by a silence like that of Death – a silence broken only by loud reports caused by the movement of the glaciers, and by thundering avalanches."

What does it matter, then, that Boeck and Keilhau broke all the sensible rules of prudence that are part of modern mountaineering? They ascended Kalvåbreen blissfully unbothered by the danger of crevasses, noting only that as the snow grew softer, they sometimes fell in almost to their necks! And Keilhau's report on the conquest of Falketind, aided by neither rope nor ice axes, is, step by haphazard step, a classic description of how *not* to climb a mountain. It is a miracle that no one got killed, – the ascent of that peak, though no challenge to an alpinist, even today is considered beyond the scope of the novice.

But now Bøyesen also seems to have been smitten by a sense of the dramatic. In the year 1822 an account was published of a trip he had made through Vettisgjelet four years earlier, in order to visit his parishioners at Vetti and Avdal. He relates: "One enters the canyon by a shaky bridge built from tree trunks . . . moving across a chasm. . . . The path is a shelf no wider than two feet, occasionally there is room for one foot only, and once in a while there is no room at all, as landslides cover the path, and one has to search for a

"Seterliv under Skagastølstindene", "Seter life near Skagastølstindene", gouache by Flintoe. In this picture, a fantasy on the theme of seter life, the silhouette of Skagastølstindene has been used as a background, detached from the rest of the Hurrungane group.

Left: Store Skagastølstind dressed in its winter "furs". Like Matterhorn, Store Skagastølstind, once conquered (by Slingsby in the year 1876), eventually became known as a fairly easy peak to trained alpinists. During the years a few not-so-trained have also been hauled to the top by patient guides. But the average tourist, even the seasoned hiker, is wise to contend him- or herself with respectfully admiring "Storen", "the big one", at a distance.

foothold among the debris. . . . Advancement became steadily more difficult and horrifying. Our progress was hampered by avalanches blocking the way . . . only by moving fast, did one avoid sliding into the abyss. At other times one was stopped short where a wall of ice covered the trail. . . . But Eivind was prepared for this. With his axe he cut a shelf, no wider than a hand, in the ice, where he put his foot, then another, where he put his other foot, and thus he proceeded until he had crossed the sheet of ice. The rest of the party had to follow in his tracks. . . . Travelling along precipices for more than half a (Norwegian) mile, we often had to cross such frozen avalanches, hanging like huge mirrors almost vertically from the top of the cliffs into the abyss. . . . One faltering step, or just a moment of dizzyness – and one would shortly be dead, crushed – ." Bøyesen also gives the first recorded description of the grandiose waterfall Vettisfossen.

Yet another man ought to be mentioned among Jotunheimen's pioneer "discoverers", though a whole generation younger than Boeck and Keilhau: the botanist, forester and huntsman Jakob Bøckmann Barth (1822–92). Barth was driven not only by the still fashionable fascination with the dramatic, he had a keen eye also for detail. And he became the troubadour of the more subdued beauty of the mountain plateaus, with "subtle, soft hues, a wonderful carpet of lovely lichens and a wide view even of the tall peaks. Yes, I confess that I love these seemingly monotonous plateaus." Among Barth's favorite haunts was Valdresflya; he writes in praise of the whitish "reindeer moss", the yellow "gold-beard", the olive "Icelandic moss" and the greyish-violet "salt-moss". And he describes the mountain plateaus as they appear in autumn: "There is no hue of red or brown, from scarlet to deep carmine to almost black, that

Vetti, destination of pastor Bøyesen on his dramatic journey through Vettisgjelet. The property, which has belonged to the same family for more than 200 years, covers some 12000 acres of which the Vettismorki forest makes up about 1/5. The rest is mostly mountain areas, in days past very valuable hunting grounds. A tractor road (5 km) through Vettisgjelet from Hjelle to Vetti was opened to traffic on June 19th 1977. The road had been constructed by the people of Årdal as a community project – some 1500 people had put in altogether about 50000 hours of work during a period of 4 years.

is not found in the carpet made up of plants common to the region at that time of the year. . . . Occasionally, walking along, one involuntarily withdraws one's foot, as if one were about to step into a pool of blood. But one discovers at once that it is only a cluster of plants of alpine bearberry. In between are spots of vivid yellow and flame red, the colours being so intense that they look like fires."

The Adventurous Ones

The account of Keilhau's and Boeck's exploits, as well as of Bøyesen's journey through Vettisgjelet, were translated and published abroad.

A prompt response were visits by a German geologist, C.F. Naumann from Dresden, who, with a medical student named Schubert, criss-crossed Southern Norway during the summers of 1821 and -22. The result was a travel book in two volumes, "Beyträge zur Kenntnis Norwegens", an introduction so thorough that a Norwegian historian (O.A. Øverland) in the year 1904 points out that it "still defends its place as an excellent and copious source of knowledge regarding Norwegian geography and living conditions". Naumann's description of Hurrungane is quite detailed – and he uses certain terms borrowed from Keilhau, to whom he refers. He also observes a phenomenon that was to baffle – and occasionally annoy – many a tourist from England and the Continent: the lack of servility characteristic of Norwegian farmers, who have never been reduced to serfdom, as have peasants of other European countries. He comments: "I admit that certain traits of the Norwegian character in the beginning struck me as unpleasant, namely a marked pride . . . this before I got to know better the way of thinking of the dwellers of Norway's mountain regions, who have valid reasons for that pride."

A party consisting of the Norwegian botanist M.N. Blytt and three artists (identified only as M., F. and L.) came to Fortun in the year 1822; they planned to climb one or more of Skagastølstindene, but poor weather prevented them from trying. Maybe the influence of the artists makes Blytt comment that the mists "tumbling back and forth" in Bergsdalen "in different circumstances would have been quite interesting". The party got as far as Turtagrø, and Blytt, who had walked ahead, was able to take in the view piecemeal, as shifting clouds allowed glimpses of the mountains.

Yet, during the next two or three decades visitors to the Jotunheimen region were few and far between. People seem to have read Keilhau's and Bøyesen's reports with shuddering delight, but generally to have felt no urge to follow their example. And Boeck never returned to Jotunheimen; Keilhau only once: In the year 1844 he stayed for a while at Spiterstulen in Visdalen, making two attempts at a first ascent of Galdhøpiggen, by then acknowledged to be Norway's loftiest peak. But foul weather turned him back.

A trickle of British tourists did, however, find their way to Norway during those years. But most of those were of the less adventurous type, keeping to the few roads that could be travelled by horse and carriage. Thus their impressions of Jotunheimen were limited to glimpses from the Fillefjell region, en route between Bergen and Oslo. Some exceptions:

In the year 1833 a widely travelled naval officer, William Breton, crossed Sognefjell from Lom to Luster – he was "doing Norway" and, travelling on foot from Romsdal to Hardanger, chose that route as the most convenient one. He was taken by surprise when he found himself in a landscape that he felt would have impressed a tourist even in Switzerland. And he included the experience in a travel book ("Scandinavian Sketches", London 1835). By then he had read up on available information concerning the area, and referred to Bøyesen's description of his trip through Vettisgjelet.

In the year 1848 another couple of British tourists visited Norway and wrote about it, Thomas Forester and M.S. Biddulph. According to the preface of their book, published in Forester's name, but including extracts from the journals of Biddulph, "free enjoyment of the beautiful scenery of this romantic country was the primary object of the excursion". The part concerning Jotunheimen is by Mr. Biddulph, who visited that region alone in the summer of the year 1848, after parting from his less adventurous friend, and returned the following year. And to Biddulph the ruggedness of Sognefjell, which he crossed from west to east, was no surprise, he knew that he was going into "one of the wildest parts of Norway". He spent a successful afternoon at Turtagrø, including a trip that seems, from his description, to have taken him and his guides up the spur of Soleitindene (of Hurrungane) in search of a herd of

reindeer – they also found "a spectacle of indescribable grandeur": "Close above us is a rocky summit, bare and pointed, in the clefts of which lie masses of snow and ice. To the south and south-west are distant views of fjelds far away, the northern extremity of the Hardanger glowing pink in the evening light. To the westward fold after fold of the snowy ridges of Sneebreen (the glacier), between which and us intervenes, unseen, the deep valley of the Sognefjord". The next day, however, "it blew a hurricane, with torrents of rain", and Biddulph crossed Sognefjell in rain and sleet, "wading through large tracts of snow" – on July 21st –. The next year he went reindeer hunting in the region between Årdal and Tyin. He bagged no deer, but again a view "inconceivably grand", looking west from Morka-Koldedalen: "The clouds occasionally concealed the whole horizon, and then breaking revealed the jagged peaks of Hurungerne (Hurrungane) above them in wild fantastic confusion. . . . Beneath a bell-shaped valley penetrated into the mountains, and was closed by a vast glacier. . . . We were disposed to linger long in view of this glorious spectacle, and it was with difficulty our guide drew us away." Somewhat further down, having arrived in the fairy-tale pine forest of Vettismorki, Biddulph finally got his chance to "linger" and made a sketch, later litographed, of Hurrungane and Stølsmaradalen.

From the 1850's and on Norwegians began in earnest to appreciate their own mountains; spearheading the first generation of Jotunheimen tourists was a medical man, Axel Arbo. Arbo's first trip, in the year 1854, was made in the region of Utladalen; after having read Bøyesen's dramatic account, he seems to have been disappointed – of which the comment may be made that he travelled out-of-season for landslides, avalanches and sheets of ice. The following year he ascended Galdhøpiggen as instigator of a group excursion, a second ascent. The guide was Steinar Sulheim, one of the three men from Lom who had made the first ascent five years earlier. Upon attaining the summit, Arbo and his party sung several patriotic songs, which was quite in keeping with the romantic nationalism of the times, and Arbo was moved to give an eloquent lecture on the view. However, his general opinion of Jotunheimen seems to be expressed in his remark, later on, that the region "everywhere gives an impression of solemnity and loneliness."

From Arbo's time on, the stream of tourists, foreign and Norwegian, increased steadily. And some of them may be termed adventurous, certainly the Englishmen Blackwell and Rathbone who came to eastern Jotunheimen to go reindeer hunting in the year 1855 – and stayed in the mountains all winter. But that strange and romantic tale shall be told elsewhere in this book.

Yet another Englishman has earned himself a well-deserved place among the "adventurous ones", even if not an early visitor: Mr. Hubert Smith, who in the year 1871 brought his gipsy friends Noah, Esmeralda and Zachariah along with him to Norway; with three donkeys those four travelled through Jotunheimen from Bøverdalen via Utladalen to Tyin. As may be expected, problems *did* arise, for instance when crossing the Utla close to that river's junction with Vetle-Utla ("Tent Life", London 1873); "There was no wading . . . We had a strong, deep, heavy current of water rushing with wild impetuosity under the overhanging rocks. High above the foaming waters, a narrow frail bridge, with a wicket and slight hand rail on each side, spanned the river. . . . Ole (Ola Røysheim, the guide) stepped across the bridge with I don't know how many pounds of baggage on his shoulders, as if he expected the whole cavalcade to follow. The donkeys looked as if they much preferred

"Hurrungerne peaks from the forest of Koldedal". Lithograph made from a sketch by M. S. Biddulph for the book "Norway in 1848 and 1849", London 1850.

Juvasshytta around 1890. When Hubert Smith and his gipsy friend Noah ascended Galdhøpiggen (with the famed Ola Røysheim as a guide, starting from Røisheim in Bøverdalen at 9 PM and arriving at the summit as the sun rose) not even a tiny cottage had been erected by Juvvatnet. And at the time of this picture, the climb still was considered quite a venture – as shown by grim looks of tourists and guide alike. Incidentally, the guide in the foreground is the famous Knut Vole.

remaining where they were. Esmeralda said we should never get over. Noah said: 'No donkey can go over such places as this, sir." "There's the other side. They must go." And without losing more time we all set to work and carried the baggage over. Then came Tarno Rye's turn; Zachariah pulled at its head, whilst ourselves and Noah pushed behind, and forced it by main strength up the stones to the wicket. It was almost over the cliff once, but we both laid hold of a hind leg each, whilst Zachariah tugged at the donkey's head. As the frail bridge shook it is lucky we did not all vanish into the chasm below. With main force the Tarno Rye was lifted on to the bridge, and finding itself there quietly allowed itself to be led by Zachariah and Ole to the other side. It was rather expected we should succeed in the same way with the other two, but they made such a resolute fight that there was considerable risk of losing one of the donkeys through the handrail at the end of the bridge. We then proposed to noose them by the head, and so drag them over. Noah further suggested that we might double the rope and pass it round the donkey's hind quarters. It was a good idea immediately adopted. The Puru Rawnee was the first. Esmeralda and Zachariah at the ends of the double rope across the bridge. Ourselves on the bridge steadying its head. Noah and Ole pushing behind. Sharp was the contest, first at the stones leading to the bridge, then at the light rails at the end of the bridge which shook under our weight as the donkey resisted. Now and again Esmeralda pulled. Zachariah pulled, and the Puru Rawnee, at length, sorely against her will, was dragged over the bridge. The Puru Rye was also soon pulled over by the same method, amid much laughter. In a few minutes the donkeys were again loaded."

The Interpreters – the Painters, Composers and Authors

It is inevitable that from this group should come some of the early Norwegian visitors to Jotunheimen.

The painters arrived first – as a matter of fact, Keilhau was an amateur painter. And of the artists in M.N. Blytt's party, visiting Jotunheimen in the year 1822, F. has been said to mean Flintoe. Anyway, Johannes Flintoe (1786–1870), a Norwegian painter of Danish ancestry, is considered the discoverer of the Norwegian alpine landscape. He was also, in keeping with the trends of his times, a painter of scenes from the life of country people; some of those paintings are romantic in the extreme, as is his rendering of "Seter life near Skagastølstindene", while others show considerable realism and a keen sense of humour. As to his contact with Jotunheimen, Claus Helberg, a Flintoe connoisseur, points out that the artist, who was also the teacher of several of Norway's best known painters of that period, acted as a "tourist guide" to his pupils – and directed a number of them to a popular artist's rendezvous, Ytre Kroken by the Luster fjord, the property of a well-known Norwegian family. And with Ytre Kroken as a base, several artists have painted in the region Fortunsdalen-Turtagrø. Later, towards the end of the 19th century and in the first decades to the 20th, Ottadalen-Bøverdalen became a favorite area of artists. And Lomseggen has been labelled "Norway's most frequently painted mountain" – rendered in pictures romantic, realistic or whatever the current style happened to be.

Several Norwegian composers have found their way to Jotunheimen; most famous is Edvard Grieg (1843–1907). It is not known when he first saw the region; he did, however, visit Røisheim in Bøverdalen in the year 1885 – he had come there from Tyin via Gjendebu. Grieg loved Jotunheimen dearly, and during a period of several years went to Turtagrø every summer. In spite

Her Royal Highness crown princess Sonja of Norway – at the summit of her country's highest mountain.

of his fragile health, he was an enthusiastic hiker who even tried a wee bit of mountain climbing. In a letter to his friend, the composer Johan Halvorsen, he wrote: "When I contemplate the possibility of a future visit to the mountains, I shudder with joy and expectation, as if it were a matter of hearing Beethoven's 10th symphony." Grieg was a romanticist, and as such sought inspiration in themes and music of his native country. Some of his compositions were directly inspired by his impressions of Jotunheimen, as was his opus 44, "Reiseminner fra fjord og fjell" ("Travel mementos from fjord and fjell"), a musical-poetical travelogue created in co-operation with the Danish poet Holger Drachmann. Incidentally, that work is not considered to be among Grieg's best. He did better when inspired by the folk music of the area. His best known source of such inspiration was Gjendine (so named because she had been born at a seter by Gjende) Slålien from Lom, who stayed summers at Gjendebu. "Gjendines bådnlåt" ("Gjendine's lullaby") and the lyrical "Hjemve" ("Longing for home") are examples – in the former, Grieg's treatment of the theme includes harmonies that are innovations within the framework of the period. But transcending those works which are traceable to specific incidents or sources is the influence that a general contact with the mountains and their folk music had upon the composer; through his compositions that influence was to become part of the mainstream of musical development in Europe.

Grieg brought the music of Jotunheimen to all the world; through another medium, literature, the area has also become part of the international scene. And the four authors that I shall mention, mirror the international literary development of the 19th century, yet make of their encounter, with that mountain area, how ever brief, something special.

The second Norwegian author known to have travelled through Jotunheimen, is Henrik Wergeland (1808–45). The first one is the later expatriate – to Denmark – Ludvig Holberg (1684–1754), "the Molière of the North", who crossed Sognefjell in his early teens, but as far as his writing is concerned, kept mum about that fact.

Though Wergeland hardly is known outside of Norway – his poetry is not easily translatable –, he has had an important influence on the cultural life of this country. He was a romanticist and a great admirer of Lord Byron; in spirit he was more an heir to the German "Sturm und Drang" movement, with its marked revolt against the injustices of society, than a representative of the more placid and introspective "new" romanticism. In the year 1832 Wergeland was hiking in Norway with a British friend, Philip Pope, and those two crossed Sognefjell from Lom to Fortun accompanied by a guide; Wergeland's evidently cloudfree view of Fannaråken, the mountain dominating the Sognefjell plateau, indicates fair weather. The trip precipitated into Wergeland's writing in an epic poem, "Spaniolen" ("The Spaniard"), concerning a Spaniard fleeing tyranny at home and meeting his death in a storm at Sognefjell, while hugging a cross with an inscription admonishing everybody to flee from that dreadful tract. As should be obvious from this, Wergeland's impression of the scenery echoes the fascination-dread that had gripped Keilhau; in his introduction to the first edition of Spaniolen (the source of all quotes below) he mentions "the terrible road . . . across the alpine desert of Sognefjell". And the guide must have given him a rather vivid description of the mountain plateau and "the glacier" – meaning Fannaråken – in a blizzard. This is Wergeland's version: "It is like an explosion, impossible to see, impossible even to stagger ahead, and snow, reeking from the top,

On the way down from Galdhøpiggen ("Piggen" for short). The picture, taken by aid of a telephoto lens, gives the false impression that a great part of Jotunheimen is within easy walking distance. Seen on the horizon from the left to the right: Torfinnstind, Kvitskartind, Mesmogtind and Langedalstind, all located in the area between Gjende and Bygdin. The peak below Torfinnstind is one of Heillstugutindene, the valley to the right of that is Urdadalen, through which goes the trail Spiterstulen – Gjendebu. Cutting across the middle of the picture is Styggehø. Foreground, right, Tverråtinden.

makes the glacier look like a volcano." As a matter of fact, that guide seems partly responsible for the mood of Spaniolen. Wergeland writes about "cairns in that mountain desert, marking the place where someone in former days got killed, or was found dead, buried by snow suddenly sweeping down from Fannaråken" – and one recognizes the tales of old, concerning people killed by robbers on this crossing; an at that time fairly recent tragedy when six men from Lom died on Sognefjell in a blizzard in the year 1813, also comes to mind, six cairns had been raised to mark the spot. It may not be so strange, then, that the impressionable poet gives this description of Fannaråken: "Seen from afar it looks like an immense coffin of the world . . . getting closer, the lid more and more seems to be broken open . . . as if the dead is awakening; and look, he is getting up – a shadowy ghost, the dreadful plume of wind-driven glacier snow." – – Come to think of it, maybe it was not so strange, either, that the average Norwegian would-be tourist to Jotunheimen needed a couple of decades to recover from that blast!

Next to pass Sognefjell in this cavalcade of authors is Peter Christen Asbjørnsen (1812–85). By profession a forester, he was one of the pioneers who made Norwegians in general conscious of the cultural heritage preserved in the folklore and traditions of their farming communities. Teaming up with the theologian (eventually he became a bishop) and poet Jørgen Moe, and inspired by the German brothers Grimm as well as by Irish work in the field of folklore, he collected folk-tales – a number of which were also published abroad. Thus Asbjørnsen spearheaded Norwegian "national-romanticism", a movement glorifying in the extreme everything inherently Norwegian. Asbjørnsen appreciated not only the occasionally rough "landscape" of the folk-tales, but also the rugged mountain scenery – he is the first Norwegian author to describe mountains as beautiful, and not at all frightening. When crossing Sognefjell from west to east in the year 1852, this was his impression: "the sun . . . threw sparkling light on the mighty glaciers that rise above the pale grey massif of Fannaråken, Hurrungane's spires and mighty bodies seemed to tremble in an airy abyss almost bluish-black, the snow of their gullies and crevices a silken veil interwoven with silver threads." Asbjørnsen (and/or Moe) also collected folk-tales in the Jotunheimen area, including one from Vågå mentioning a few "troll"s – and the foreigners who had been trapping falcons in the region.

The Vinje monument (sculptor: Ståle Kyllingstad) by Eidsbugarden, the lodge named for Vinje's Eidsbu cottage at the eastern end of Bygdin.

Third among our authors is a poet who, like Wergeland, is practically unknown abroad: Aasmund Olavsson Vinje (1818–70). Vinje, like Grieg, loved Jotunheimen, and returned again and again. He was the one who gave to the mountain massif its name, inspired by Keilhau's "Jotunfjeldene" and in allusion to the "Jotun-heimr", "Home of the giants", of old Norse mythology; he also gave to Boeck's and Keilhau's Morka-Koldedalstind its present name of Falketind (Falcon Peak). Yet, when Vinje first visited the area, in his early forties, he was famed mainly as a journalist whose wit and acid pen had made him many enemies. Vinje had been a country boy; he was a man who had known poverty, and who had suffered acutely from the ridicule heaped upon him by the capital's high society for his lack of polish. His encounter with Jotunheimen became a symbolic reunion with the mountains of his boyhood, and released the pent-up romantic in this otherwise sarcastic realist – Vinje became the instigator of a Norwegian trend that has later been termed "mountain-romanticism". He describes thus his first close-up look at Jotunheimen (from the mountains above Bøverdalen): "The sun sank into the ice-ocean and painted snow and glaciers and peaks fiery red. A full moon rose

Jotunheimen has been the main subject of several Tourist Association Yearbooks. And the cover of the 1928 book (the picture to the right), showing Glittertind, has become a classic of its kind. To Vinje that peak was the most beautiful in Jotunheimen, and many tend to agree with him. And as a symbol of national and mountain romanticism it has outdone the higher, but less spectacular Galdhøpiggen. What, then, could be more appropriate than to ascend Glittertind in celebration of the Tourist Association's 60th Anniversary in 1928? – a girl in national costume carried a Norwegian flag with the Association's emblem to the summit. And the event was duly recorded (picture above) by Norway's foremost landscape photographer of the period, Anders Beer Wilse.

Overleaf: Galdhøpiggen seen from Glittertind.

above Glittertind as if struggling for power with the dying sun, which kept paling until fleeing even from Galdhøpiggen, its flames heading for the heavens through the veil of clouds." When stating that the joy brought by that view would remain with him throughout his life, he spoke the mere truth. And it seems as if communion with the mountain world somehow counterbalanced his ofttimes bitterness and brusqueness towards his fellow men. Eventually, with some friends, Vinje built a cottage at Eidsbu, by the western end of Bygdin – Hubert Smith visited the place when he travelled with his gipsy companions, calling it the "poet's house" and giving a glowing description of the view across the expanse of the lake. Incidentally, that lake was to cause Vinje some anxious moments. Once when he and his friends were rowing from its eastern to its western end, the winds were quite strong. One of the party, used to boats and the sea, rigged a mast and sail from walking sticks and blankets. As they were coasting westwards before the wind, Vinje, definitely no sailor, was hollering that they were "risking their lives" and "It's nobody's loss if *you* drown like whelps. But *I* have a mission, so pull that sail down at once!" Vinje spent two happy summers at Eidsbu. But the third summer, that of the year 1870, found him dying in an Oslo hospital. "Do you remember the view from Skineggen that morning?" he said to a friend visiting him. "When the white mists were dispersing around Skagastølstindene, and Koldedalsbreene were pure gold in the glorious sunlight. – My oh my, that I shall not come there this summer!" He fell silent, then went on: "But when I'm in my coffin, then my spirit shall find its home there, among the peaks, and I shall rest on Falketind, enhanced by the view of the land –." Finally Vinje could stand it no longer. He got up and left for his mountains, but died on the way.

Last among these authors: the playwright Henrik Ibsen (1828–1906), who hardly needs any introduction. As far as Jotunheimen is concerned, Ibsen was a "one-crossing-of-Sognefjellet"man; he travelled from Lom to Fortun in the year 1862. The playwright, not yet appreciated in his native land, had been denied a grant for which he had applied – as a consolation he had been given a much smaller sum, for the purpose of collecting folk-tales and -songs, which was the occasion for his journey. But the trip was not Ibsen's first encounter with Norway's mountains; he had previously written poetry indicating his familiarity and fascination with that world. In a poem written in the year 1860 he had already established some of the symbolism that marks his later works; to a huntsman his free life among the mountains becomes a symbol of freedom from the narrow-mindedness of "the valley" and the shackles of traditional life and religion – and a way to his God. Accordingly, the playwright brought along with him to Sognefjell certain pre-conceived ideas – yet the crossing left him with impressions that may be traced in his work till the end of his life. But Ibsen never just reported his experiences; he assimilated them, made them part of his own "inner landscape", and gave them new life in his plays. Thus, according to tradition, Ibsen and his guide ran into foul weather and had to seek shelter in a stone hut in the vicinity of Fannaråken. And here are the first lines of the play Brand (1866):

(In a fog). Farmer, walking with Brand: "Hi, stranger, don't go so fast! Where are you?" Brand: "Here." Farmer: "You'll get lost. The fog is getting so heavy that I can hardly see the length of my staff." The farmer's son: "Father, a crack in the snow!" Farmer: "Crevasses!" Brand: "And we have lost every trace of the path." Farmer (shouting): "Stop, man! God's death! Right here the glacier is just a thin crust! Do not step on that snow!" Brand:

"I hear a waterfall." Farmer: "A stream has hollowed the glacier out; here is an abyss too deep to fathom, it could swallow you as well as us."

Now, there is no glacier to cross on the Sognefjell path. There are, however, permanent snow-drifts. And Ibsen uses the word "bre" ("glacier") rather loosely, meaning both. He probably also, like Wergeland, made use of his guide as a source of information. But the landscape of Brand, though obviously inspired by that of Sognefjell and Fortun, is by no means identical to it; to Ibsen symbolism was vastly more important than topographical features. And those opening lines of Brand have already introduced two symbols that recur in his works: the mists and the glacier; further on in that opening scene is found two more: the avalanche and the "ice church" – the latter a special feature of Brand. It is highly probable that Ibsen had experienced an avalanche on Sognefjell, though at a safe distance – his description of one, in Brand's last scene, is quite realistic. But as to the ice church – any similarity

Sognefjell. Fannaråken in the center of the picture.

The author Henrik Wergeland's terrible "coffin of the world", Fannaråken, has been domesticated to the point where it is topped with a meteorological station as well as a cottage belonging to the Tourist Association. The station has till now been manned on a year-round basis, and during winters – they are long on Fannaråken – visitors are few indeed. Minimum temperatures are below freezing on the average 320 days a year, and most days are foggy. That cold and fog may also rule inside, is indicated by the story of two meteorologists who got into a quarrel during their stay there; they quit talking to each other and only exchanged notes when that was absolutely necessary!

to the Sognefjell plateau is lacking. Here is the description given in Brand: "a frozen tarn is floor and bench, the crest of snow is arching out way up, like a roof from the top of the rocky wall», above, pointing towards the heavens, is "Svartetind" ("Black Peak") – and «Never go there! A gust of wind has often caused an avalanche – ."

A glimpse into one of Hurrungane's wild valleys, or the tales of his guide, could have made Ibsen's fantasy spin. Yet, there exists another description of another part of Jotunheimen, one that contains all the elements of Brand's ice church, and one that Ibsen very likely had read: Keilhau's account of Jotunheimen's "discovery". Here are found, looking north from Kalvåhøgda, avalanche-spawning snowdrifts protruding "like a roof" above the "steep walls" of a "dreadful valley", and, in Koldedalen, "a tiny. . .cold lake", the "black spire" of Falketind "rising towards frightening heights" and a "silence like that of Death", broken by "thundering avalanches".

Brand, a zealot who has preached the gospel of a jealous God demanding "all or nothing", and has been chased by his congregation from the valley, dies in his ice church, buried by an avalanche – when he finally realizes that his efforts to save the world have been misguided and vain.

In the companion play to Brand, Peer Gynt (1867), is found not only the mountain symbolism, but also the world of Jotunheimen's folk-tales and legends – which, incidentally, has made that play suffer a curious fate in Norway. On the surface it is a satire on the excesses of Norwegian national-romanticism. Yet by-and-by the romanticists overlooked the satire part, embracing the play so eagerly that it was practically strangled in the process.

Almost a century was to pass before Norwegians began to grasp the fact that Ibsen had *not* written a romantic play about life in the country, but a witty and at the same time deadly serious "play of everyman" – and that the trappings, even the satire, were of minor importance. Peer Gynt, too, encounters the peak, pointing towards heaven, and the avalanche – though in his fantasy – at the crucial moment when, after fumbling through the mists, he finally has accepted his own unimportance, his nothingness: "I want to rise, to ascend the highest peak, once more to see the sunrise, to look, until I'm weary, at the promised land. Then better to perish under heaps of snow; they may write above: Here *no one* is buried –". But while the somber Brand must die at the moment of his enlightenment, to the happy-go-lucky Peer the very same experience opens a possible way towards new life.

The mists, the peak and the avalanche return in the very last scene of Ibsen's very last play, "Når vi døde vågner" ("When we dead awaken"). Here the main characters, a sculptor and his once model, whom he has loved and left desolate for the sake of his art, realize that they have both gone through life like "living dead". Awakened now, they are heading "through the mists" towards the "peak of the promised land", into the sunrise – and are buried by an avalanche.

Peeking down the steep Berdalen into Fortunsdalen, the inspiration of Henrik Ibsen's narrow, dark valley in "Brand". To the left, high above that valley, lies the farm Furås (mentioned on page 149) – and according to Slingsby "a lovely place it is too, once you have got there".

Tourism — from Guides to Autos

Development in Jotunheimen during the last century has mainly been marked by two trends: the influx of tourists and the effects of a utilitarian view regarding any piece of land as an economic resource to be developed. To some degree those trends have served one another; tourism has brought economic gain to individuals and groups, and roads built in connection with hydroelectric power projects have opened the area to new groups of tourists. But in general a conflict of interest has emerged, a conflict that has steadily become clearer as the philosophy and science of ecology has "come of age". And an open struggle erupted when conservationists were jolted awake by the prospect of seeing the entire region used for electric power purposes. Now a question has also been raised as to how much tourism the area can take without losing its character of being a wilderness.

And the challenge presently offered by Jotunheimen to Norway's politicians as well as to people at the grass-roots level, is that of keeping materialism from running amuck – eventually that of maintaining ecological balance within an area overrun by a large number of visitors.

Problems of this sort were not even anticipated by early tourists. To them the challenge of Jotunheimen was that of coping with life in a wilderness – a challenge which, incidentally, still can be very real. Hardly a year goes by without people losing their lives in that mountain area; freezing to death in blizzards, being buried by avalanches, tumbling into crevasses, falling off the edge of cliffs.

But, going back to when it all began – :

Of Guides and Reindeer

The first known guide in Jotunheimen is Ola Urden, the Valdres huntsman whose services Boeck and Keilhau had secured. Ola did not shrink from climbing with those two madcaps to the top of Morka-Koldedalstind/Falke-

Tourists on Sognefjell around the year 1890, when people still walked that path. Which, incidentally, they continued to do for quite a few years to come; the first motor road was opened to traffic in the year 1938. Photo: K. Knudsen.

tind. He did, however, refuse to go along when Keilhau emotionally insisted that he would not return by the route of ascent. Ola sensibly stated that they knew it would be possible also to descend that way, while they knew nothing of any other route. And as Ola staunchly stuck to his point or view, and Keilhau would not change his mind, the three parted company – eventually each made the descent on his own.

The next traveller to name his guide, is Biddulph; Sjur, the farmer of Svanheim in Årdal, who accompanied him and his friends reindeer hunting, gets this testimonial: "He was a good-humoured fellow, and entered into our plans with much readiness, though there was an air of great independence about him." And that independence seems to have been characteristic of Norwegian guides, from Ola Urden's time till this day. As a matter of fact, the most famous of them all hardly considered himself to be a guide, but a teacher and friend to the two Englishmen who turned up at his door.

His name was Jo Tjøstolsson Kleppe (1794–1884), and he was a great-grandson of the famed Vågå hunter "Strong-Tjøstol" Kleppe, mentioned earlier in this book. Losing his parents early, Jo grew up in the home of his mother's sister, at Heringstad in Heidalen. During one period of his life he therefore was known, after the name of that farm, as Jo Heringstad. And from Heringstad had come another legendary huntsman, also mentioned above, "Big-Heringstad".

Jo had no trouble living up to the tradition of both names. He was a crack shot and showed almost unbelievable stamina in the pursuit of deer. Furthermore, he knew every inch of a wide terrain with Gjende at its centre, and he was so well acquainted with the habits of the deer that he could "think like a reindeer", and thus always knew where to find them. He is supposed to have

View of Hurrungane from Oscarshaug, "Oscar's mound", named for prince Oscar Fredrik, later king Oscar II of Norway and Sweden. The prince crossed Sognefjell in the year 1860 (as had his brother king Carl XV four years previously); he described the trip in lyrical terms and with great enthusiasm. Oscarshaug, alt. 1168 m, is located very close to the present-day road. In the center of the picture: Dyrhaugsryggen – a name that may be literally translated to "the deer-mound ridge", and thus indicates hunting in the area.

shot 500–600 deer, mostly large bucks. He also lived up to the huntsmen's reputation as outsiders to people of their farming communities. Many were a bit scared of him, and by most he was regarded as a rather ungodly person. For Jo, a homespun philosopher, was a fierce rebel against the church and the clergy – a rationalist heir to the Age of Enlightenment. His library was not large, but he squeezed his few books for all they were worth and a bit more, and then took off on his own. It has been said of him, somewhat pompously, that "reason was his God and nature his temple". He was also a man who preferred the company of people who catered to his vanity. And he was moody and could be on the brusque side.

To posterity Jo Kleppe/Heringstad – and eventually, when he bought the small farm Brurusten in Heidalen in the year 1850, Jo Brurusten – has become known as Jo Gjende; this because his headquarters for years were a cottage at the eastern end of that lake. Incidentally, the cottage he built around the year 1840 to replace a ramshackle hut, is still found there, not far from Gjendesheim lodge.

Jo Gjende was a man turned 60 – and somewhat depressed because his attempts at getting a wife to Brurusten had brought no result – when two young and adventurous Englishmen, both scions of wealthy families, turned up at Gjende with a hunter-guide from the French town of Chamonix. Quite likely they had read Mr. Biddulph's account of reindeer hunting in Jotunheimen – though of what use a specialist on chamois hunting in the Alps might be in that connection, is an open question. It does, however, seem as if the two, John E. Blackwell, age 22, and a Mr. Rathbone, almost immediately hit it off with Jo, for whom they evidently soon felt great admiration. They stayed on through the autumn and into the winter with him at his Gjende cottage – hunting, fishing and mountain climbing, ice bathing and drinking blood from the newly killed deer. Especially Rathbone seems to have been a man who wanted to try everything. According to local traditions, perpetuated by indignant people, his experiments even included eating Jotunheimen frogs – hardly as tasty as their French cousins – and ermine fried in butter! The pair also paid their respects at the Lom parsonage, at that time a gathering place for tourists. In her memoirs the minister's daughter gives a rather striking description of Mr. Rathbone: he turned up at the parsonage bareheaded, a woolen thread around his head to keep his long, blond hair out of his eyes; in spite of his delicate features and melancholy blue eyes he seemed to be a through-and-through sceptic who scorned most of his fellow men. The two learned the local dialect, including a splendid selection of swearwords, from Jo. And when, at a Christmas party in Vågå, young Blackwell met the most beautiful girl of that community, he fell head over heels in love. Her name was Mari Svee, and he married her that spring, bought a farm, Klones, in Vågå and settled there for a few years – exactly for how long is not known. Aasmund Olavsson Vinje visited him at Klones in the year 1861; he seems to have left for England shortly after that, taking his Norwegian wife with him. As to Rathbone, he spent a second winter with Jo by Gjende before he left Norway for good.

The Blackwells' connection with Vågå did, however, bring several of their circle to the Gjende area. Among them was John Blackwell's brother, who leased fishing rights in Russvatn, and came to Norway hunting and fishing regularly until his death (in the year 1915). To Jo the British visitors seem to have been a most welcome change-of-pace during the last decades of his life. And so was his friendship with some other Jotunheimen tourists, notably the

Left: Two churches, each by a gateway to Jotunheimen.
Above: Lom center with that community's medieval church, seen from Leshø's steep slope. Lom has been a gateway to Jotunheimen in more than a geographic sense. The parson during the years 1855-63, Julius Aars, was hospitable in the extreme, and an enthusiast who encouraged everybody to visit Jotunheimen. Axel Arbo, Ibsen, Vinje, prince Oscar Fredrik, all came to his parsonage – as did Blackwell and Rathbone.
Below: Fortun. Serenity and the bounty of summer in a valley that belies its reputation of being dark.

forester and huntsman Jakob Bøckmann Barth, the man who wrote so enthusiastically about the mountain plateaus of the area. Incidentally, Barth has also written a biography of Jo Gjende.

From the 1860's and on to the turn of the century another area frequented by British hunters was Årdal. Among the Englishmen to favour that region were lord Sherbroke, the lawyer Charles Burrows and Mr. Thomas Turner Farley. Their guide and friend was the farmer and huntsman Sjur Ingebrigtsson Eldegard, descendant of the Jahas Eldegard mentioned earlier in this book as the first Jotunheimen hunter known by name. Sjur was no meaner a hunter than Jo Gjende – he, too, is credited with having shot more than 500 reindeer, most of them bucks. And, like Jo, he despised the magazine guns that came into use towards the end of the 1800's. In addition to his own extensive hunting territory, he leased hunting rights from 5 other Årdal farms, so that he could use most of the Årdal land east of Utladalen; he also built

Sunrise – looking south-east from the summit of Fannaråken. In the background right: Hjelledalstind, Stølsnostind, Falketind; left: Uranostind, Sagi. Below the DNT cottage: the Keisaren pass – part of Fortun's hunting grounds. The mountain of which a slope is barely visible as a dark shadow in the lower right-hand corner of the picture, is Semmelnosi, its name derived, as in Semmeltind, from "simle" meaning female reindeer.

stone huts to house the hunters to whom he sub-let those rights – l
"Engelskbua" ("The English hut") at Sletterust in Moadalen, 7 × 5
containing two rooms. Sjur's Englishmen were well liked in Årdal. Acc
to tradition, they were usually in high spirits and during evenings in t
were joking and singing. Only occasionally, when weather had been
unpleasant and hunting poor, one or another might be noticeably deje
Once, after such a day, one of the men ran back and forth outside the
flapping his arms to get warm and shouting: "Never again to the No
Never to the North I have said. The North is too cold!"

Best known among the hunter-guides from Valdres is Gudbrand Andriss
Skattebu (1836–1925). He came from Øystre Slidre, but during the yea
1875–99 he was host of the Norwegian Tourist Association's lodge Tvinneha
gen by Tyin. Gudbrand was a busy man. In addition to shooting and trappin
he worked as a farmer, a tailor, a carpenter and a butcher – he also was activ

Lom Church
Julius Aars

in community affairs. An during his time at Tvinnehaugen, he not only took people hunting and tended to the welfare of his guests, but acted as a regular guide, taking tourists to Vetti, Eidsbu og Gjendebu, and to the top of nearby mountains. Consequently his hunting time was limited, and compared with the number of reindeer shot by Jo Gjende and Sjur Eldegard, his tally of about 150 does not measure up. He would, however, happily have spent more time going after the deer, especially during his Tvinnehaugen period.

One story from his diary concerns two Englishmen for whom he acted as a guide from Tyin to Vetti. In Koldedalen, while the tourists were busy admiring mountains and glaciers, Gudbrand spied some reindeer, and, as he writes: "Of course it is marvellous to get the chance of being a guide to great and mighty foreigners, but I would gladly have exchanged them for those deer!" It so happened, as the party was getting on towards Fleskedalen through rather rough terrain, that Gudbrand tripped and skinned his ankle. And though he made nothing of it, his charges could not help noticing that he was dragging his foot and bleeding. Being of a kind sort, they had a conference between them, then made Gudbrand draw them a map of the rest of the way to Vetti, paid him off, and dismissed him. To Gudbrand's delight the condition of his foot improved markedly as he was heading back towards those deer –.

Gudbrand also tells a couple of stories about another kind of reindeer hunt, one with traditions probably dating back to the Stone Age. One of them: "A man came into the house at Tvinnehaugen shouting: Reindeer are swimming in the lake! . . . We ran to the boat, bringing a couple of long ropes, and rowing as hard as we could we managed to get in front of the deer, between them and land. We kept manoeuvering so that we tired them out while preventing them from going ashore. Then we threw ropes around the horns of two bucks, pulled them to the boat, knocked them out with a birch pole and killed them with our knives while they were in the water."

Before leaving the reindeer, I shall let the maybe gentlest hunter to stalk in Jotunheimen, the British alpinist William C. Slingsby, tell about a hunt; his story gives an idea of the rigors involved. "The spoor (track) led us over a ridge and into Simleholet, in which is a very pretty little glacier. After advancing over some moraine we saw the herd, which, with the exception of their sentinel, were sleeping on the snow at the end of the cirque and just below a huge black precipice. The wind favoured me, but nothing else, and well do I remember that interesting but most difficult and futile stalk; how I crawled along the steep mountain-side, inch by inch, hour after hour, up and down, over dry rocks and along wet shallow gullies, with my rifle sometimes in front of me, sometimes behind; and how, when I had all but arrived within shot, I knocked down a tiny, flat stone, about the size of a five-shilling piece, which only rolled ten or a dozen feet, and the alarm was given at once. The herd raced over the little skar (notch) under Simletind and they were gone. It was a beautiful sight, well worth the hours of toil, and well worth the final disappointment too."

But Slingsby brings to mind a different kind of guide: the alpinist guide, who shall be mentioned further on in this book. Yet there was another group of guides who, though also guides for hunters and alpinists, primarily were guides for ordinary tourists. Those men mainly came from Lom, possibly because Galdhøpiggen and Glittertind, both easily climbed and both favorite goals of tourists, were located in that area. I shall mention a few names: Steinar Sulheim, one of the three who had made the first ascent of Galdhøpiggen, Knut O. Vole, whose story shall be told in another article, and the most famous of them all, Ola H. Røysheim – who acted as a guide for, among many others, Hubert Smith and his party of gipsies. Mr. Smith gives Ola Røysheim this testimonial: "in every way trustworthy, and thoroughly acquainted with an extensive region of mountain land. . . . he never makes difficulties, speaks English well, will do the best he can to save expenses, talks little, but to the purpose, is always ready for start at whatever hour you name." As a matter of fact, Ola, who also spoke German passably well and had a smattering of French, had spent a winter in England to learn the language of most of his foreign tourists. And a well-known English guide-book of the period, "How to see Norway" by John R. Campbell (London 1871), remarks on Ola Røysheim's knowledge of botany and mineralogy, and calls him a "justly celebrated guide".

As a rule guides became superfluous when reindeer hunting ceased and tourists learned to manage on their own by the aid of maps, compass and marked trails. But some guiding is still done in Jotunheimen: across glaciers and on mountains not in the alpine class, yet too difficult to tackle by the average tourist without expert help.

On Map-makers and Maps

The year 1826 is *the* historical year as far as Jotunheimen map-making is concerned, marking the beginning of the first topographical survey of the region. That year a young army captain, Theodor Broch, triangulated parts

From Sjodalen – Jo Gjende's territory.

of the area, then returned the following year and again in the year 1838. He later contributed a very detailed, but unfortunately very boring, description of Jotunheimen to a new edition (1840) of a then well-known topographical work on Norway. It is doubtful that his account penetrated beyond a narrow circle of geographers.

Broch's work was carried on in the early 1840's by Harald N.S. Wergeland, a cousin of the author Henrik Wergeland. In connection with his surveys, and accompanied by Hans Sletten from Lom, Wergeland made the first recorded ascent of Glittertind (in the year 1842). Prior to that (in the year 1841) he had established by observations made from Lomseggen that Galdhøpiggen is Jotunheimens highest peak – though the top of Glittertind's glacier, now some 20 m, then more, above that mountain proper, was and probably still is the highest *point*. Wergeland also met Jo Gjende, from whom he no doubt gleaned valuable topographical information, and he became one of Jo's friends.

A fairly serviceable map of eastern Jotunheimen was published in the year 1849, but work in the rugged western area lagged behind. When a map of that region was still in the preparatory stages in the year 1870, the newly founded Norwegian Tourist Association stepped in and financed a survey of its own, in the main based on existing trigonometric points; the result was a rough, yet usable map, and a description of the area published the following year.

Geography in the field: where best to cross an un-bridged stream? From days of old the name Spranget, meaning "the leap", has been used for places where it just *might* be possible to make it across – . An example is Ridderspranget mentioned on page 152; "ridder" means "knight".

Boating on Bygdin. (For the interpretation of that lake's name see page 140.)

The Norwegian Office of Geographical Survey subsequently issued maps covering all of Jotunheimen, this in connection with work on a series projected to cover the whole country. And Johan Hertzberg, who began his surveying of Jotunheimen in the year 1871, made a number of first recorded ascents of fairly easily climbed peaks.

Though how easy it was to climb them under the circumstances, may be a matter of discussion. Those surveyors of old brought along a cumbersome and heavy load: their theodolites, an instrument necessary to measure height and horizontal distances – even when an old-fashioned theodolite was dismantled, its heaviest part weighed some 40 kg. And mounting one could take a couple of hours. The Geographic Survey Office's old descriptions of trigonometric points read like a tourist guide-book, giving advice as to where to get a pack-horse, how far the horse could be used, where to set up camp, where to get water and firewood, and include information regarding the distance from the camp to the "point", usually located on some summit, and descriptions of possible routes. Local men were engaged to help carry, also to build cairns at those "points". – And that was only the first part of the operation. The second, done by different people, was drawing the maps, which also took place on the spot. The map-maker was sitting at his surveyor's plane, a kind of table which had been carried to a suitable place from where 3–4 trigonometric points could be seen and used as a basis for his work.

It certainly is understandable that the early map-makers shrunk from tackling a really rugged area, like the Hurrungane massif. Neither did the man who drew the Tourist Association's map of western Jotunheimen go very

Geographic panorama of Øystre Slidre, Valdres, towards the mountains around Bygdin. Bitihorn, characteristic sentinel of this south-eastern entrance to Jotunheimen, is seen in the upper right-hand corner of the picture. Photo by Wilse.

deeply into that particular region – he stated that it would be uninteresting for tourists anyway, as there was nothing but rocks and snow.

Yet the first map of the entire Jotunheimen area was again financed by the Tourist Association (in the year 1910), as part of an effort to make hikers independent of guides. The man who made it did, however, depend on work done by the people of the Geographic Survey Office.

And map-making is still going on in Jotunheimen, now by help of aerial photography and all other modern aids. But the area does not top the Office's list of firsts in the new series of maps, scale 1:50000, projected to cover all of Norway – topping that list are regions which have not, till now, been covered by even serviceable maps; the first Jotunheimen section of the series is not scheduled to go on sale until the year 1979. As a matter of fact, the Jotunheimen maps being issued today on the scale 1:50000 are mere blowups of the older series, scale 1:100000, published during the first half of this century (later reprints brought up to date as to roads and the like) and partly based on surveys dating back to Hertzberg and the early 1870's. And, with all due respect to Hertzberg and the other people responsible for that series, flaws are not improved by being enlarged. The general map of the whole region, scale 1:250000, is based on that same series.

However, three very good maps of eastern, central and western Jotunheimen respectively, a special series, scale 1:50000, were issued during the late 1930's, based on then recent suveys. Though still available, they have not been brought up to date lately, and may offer the user some surprises. However, in combination with the up-to-date, blown-up series, they give fairly good coverage. Unfortunately the special series does not take in the entire region; a large section to the south and east is left out – .

What's in a Name?

Reading a map with the names in a foreign language, can be frustrating – the "map-reader's dictionary" supplied on page 200 may be of some help.

One piece of information about Norwegian grammar is also relevant to map-reading: the definite article is suffixed to the noun. Furthermore, the language uses three genders, masculine, feminine and neuter, and that article commonly takes these forms: m. "-en" (ex. dal – dalen, bekk – bekken), f. "-a" (ex. li – lia), and n. "-et" (ex. vatn – vatnet, tjern – tjernet). Plural has these variants: m. "-ane" or "-ene" (ex. dalane, bekkene), f. "-ene" (ex. liene) and n. "-a" or "-ene" (ex. vatna, tjernene). On Jotunheimen maps are also found a number of variants occuring in local dialects – singular suffixes "-n", "-i", "-e", plural suffixes "-ein", "-an" "-adn" etc. But all that is a quite complicated matter on which has been written many a thesis, and, in this connection, is better left alone.

A number of place-names are, however, interesting beyond a mere translation that can be made with a knowledge of modern Norwegian. In their way they tell a story of the people who gave to the rivers, the mountains, the valleys those particular names. But interpreting them requires a combined knowledge of old Norse, of the history of the Norwegian language and of modern dialects, something which few people possess. Our guide on a mini-tour through the "landscape" of Jotunheimen names will therefore be an acknowledged authority on the matter, Lars Ekre. I must admit, though, that I do not know for sure what information I have from his writings and what from our chats on the topic.

The youngest layer of names in Jotunheimen has been given by tourists during the last century and a half – to those belong Vinje's creations Jotunheimen and Falketind and such obviously new names as Keilhaus topp (top) and Slingsbys bre. They furthermore include the collection "of animals and kitchen tools" that have been assigned Smørstabbtindane (a main feature of the view east from Sygnefjell/Sognefjell): Kniven (the knife), Geita (the goat), Saksa (the scissors), Skeia (the spoon), Kalven (the calf), Lillebjørn (little bear) and Storebjørn (big bear). The word "pigg", "peak", also is of fairly recent origin in the area; "tind" is an older term.

But some of the older names, too, have obviously been given by travellers. For instance, Høgvaglen means "the high cairn", and is the name of the pass at the highest point of the Leirdalen – Gjendebu trail. A number of nearby names, Høgvageltind, Høgvageltjørnen, Høgvagelbrean must also have been given by people frequenting that path.

Demonstrating its "traveller" origin as well as the name's own tendency to travel, is "Gald-" in Bøverdalen; "gald" means a spot difficult to pass, or a steep path. The word is found also in Galdeberg by Bygdin, where the path has to leave the shore and climb into the mountains, in Galden at Tyin's southern end, in Galdeberg at Sygnefjell and in Fortunsgalden, the old footpath from the farm Berge to Fortun. Galde (dial. Geidde) in Bøverdalen first lent its name to the farm just down the valley, Galde, then, through that, to the community Galdbygden (bygd means rural community), to Galdlie and Galdhøe, respectively the mountainside and the mountain south of that farm, and finally to Galdhøpiggen, earlier known as Galdhøtind. Incidentally, Jotunheimen's second and third highest peaks Glittertind and store Skagastølstind, also have names that have "moved up" from the valleys. Glittertind is named for the river Glitra (the glittering), running into Visa –

Glitra also has lent its name to Glitteroksle and Glitterbrean. And the name Skagastølstindane originates at Skagen (meaning a point of land), a Fortun farm; the Skagen seter got the name Skagastølen, and the mountains above that became Skagastølstindane – there are also a Skagastølsdalen and a Skagastølsbreen. Those people certainly got milage out of a name! And obviously, they were valley dwellers, not alpinists, which is also shown by the fact that rivers lent their names to their lakes or glaciers of origin, and to peaks.

Other names bear witness to hunting in the area; typical are Bukkebotn (bukk here means reindeer buck) and Simleholet (simle means female reindeer). Less obvious is the river name Bessa. It is, however, derived from an old Norse word for bear, "bersi", and means Bear river. And from that name is derived Bessvatn, Besshø and Besseggje (Besseggen).

Still another type constitutes, in effect, geographic clocks. The dwellers of a farm or seter used the peaks or hills in the vicinity to mark time according to the sun's movement during the day – a very practical system, really, prior to the age of wrist watches. And, returning to Galdbygden in Bøverdalen: with a farm in that community as the center is found a series of those names. At 6 AM the sun is above Morgonverdkampen (old Norse "morgunverðr" means «morning meal"), at 9 AM above Dugurdmålkampen (from old Norse

Left: The guidepost at Spiterstulen (meaning the seter by the river Spitra). Fortunately most names are easier to figure out than those!

Right: Gjende at dawn. And the view certainly is enchanced by the fact that the lake is – straight. Incidentally, the ancient Norse word that is supposed to be the origin of the name Gjende, "gandr", meaning "rod", also had the meaning "magic wand" – .

"dagverðr" meaning "day meal"), at 3 PM above Nonshø (old Norse "non" is derived from latin "nona (hora)", the 9th hour reckoned from 6 AM). Names of that type are fairly common, though mostly known only in the small area where they are relevant. Yet some, especially many a Nonshø or -haug, have become official names, found on maps, and it is then possible to pinpoint the farm or seter from which the name was originally given.

But Jotunheimen has an even older group of names, and an age of at least one and a half millennium is indicated by their linguistic background. Prime examples are the names of the three large lakes Gjende, Bygdin and Tyin. The names have been interpreted to mean, respectively, "the straight (one)", "the bent (one)" and "the forked (one)". And the people who gave those names to the three lakes must have had more of an overall picture of Jotunheimen's geography than people of the past are generally credited with – they evidently climbed high as well as travelled wide – .

The Tourist's own Club

The Norwegian Tourist Association (Den Norske Turistforening, DNT for short) was founded in the year 1868. And the man who promoted the idea, Thomas J. Heftye, probably had been inspired by his first two encounters with Jotunheimen, though in different ways. In the year 1854 he crossed Sognefjell in glorious weather. Then, five years later, he experienced some of the problems that might faze a Jotunheimen tourist. With a friend he climbed Bitihorn in driving rain by a route unnecessarily difficult – they had missed the easier one. Arriving at Bygdin they found the guides, with whom they had made an appointment, so threatening that they paid and dismissed them. They proceeded to row the length of that lake in a boat so leaky that constant bailing was necessary. And it was still raining. At Eidsbu they spent the night in a miserable drovers' hut – evidently the very one that the drover Kristian Heltne so gladly abandoned in favour of comfortable quarters in Vinje's house. A hiker, who had also spent a night there, bitterly complains that it is the worst of the awful drovers' huts by Bygdin: "a stone hut . . . with a door like that of a dog house, so that one had to crawl in on all fours. There is no window and, of course, an earthen floor . . . (there is) a hole in the wall to be filled with twigs each time one wants a fire. All smoke gathers inside the hut, and everybody has to go outside until the smoke has found its way out through the door. By then the heat inside is tropical." The day following Heftye and his friend made their way along the shore of Tyin on unsaddled horses, still in driving rain – .

Heftye evidently made up his mind to do something about the state of affairs. As DNT's first president, an office he held until his death in the year 1886, he energetically stepped into action. And though Jotunheimen is only one of DNT's project areas, it seems to have been Heftye's favourite.

DNT had three main problems to tackle in Jotunheimen.

First of all, the area was not easily accessible in those days. so the association contributed to the building and improvement of roads, and engaged in an unfortunate venture with the purpose of acquiring a boat that could carry passengers on Tyin. The boat eventually got as far as Bygdin, where it remained; the transport across to Tyin proved too expensive.

Next there was the problem of housing. In addition to drovers' and hunters' huts there were seters, but those were certainly not built with tourists in mind. I quote William C. Slingsby, who gathered his experiences of Jotunheimen

Grasviksetrene by Svartberget in Øvre Sjodalen. Those seters, known by tourists of a century ago, were struck by an avalanche; Grasviksetrene of today lie in a safer spot. The drawing is by Kristen Holbø and is part of the work "Norge i det 19. Aarhundre", "Norway in the 19th century".

Vinstervatnet – dusk of evening. The seters in the foreground are Lykkjestølane.

seter life during the 1870's: "A sæter sæl usually has two rooms, an outer and an inner one, as well as a half open porch, where is the corner fireplace where large pans of milk and cream are boiled over a slow log-fire. The first room has one or two small glass windows, usually with several broken panes stopped up with rags or paper; two or three wooden stools; a table, which probably lets down against the wall, a rustic bed . . . (with) rough cross pieces laid over the framework, and juniper twigs, heather, or dwarf willow or birch laid on, and possibly also some hay or reindeer moss. Then come the bed-clothes, the variety of which is certainly surprising. Rugs, sacks, sheets, and sheep or goat skins are commonly found. The pillow is stuffed with hay or occasionally feathers. The inner room usually is very small and full of shelves on which are placed innumerable bowls of milk, cream and thick curds or cheeses in various stages of manufacture. In the poorer sæters the porch is absent and the fireplace is in the same room as the bed." He also comments: "It is well to know that in asking for food or a night's lodging at a sæter, one is asking for a favour. The girls will, without hesitation, almost always give up their bed, and sleep uncomfortably crowded together in another hut. They will give you the best fare that they can" – he mentions the milk and cream dishes commonly served at the seters – . "It may not suit every one, but, for a time, it suits me well." And he has noticed how busy the budeie is: "She may keep you waiting for an hour until she has finished milking, before she can attend to your wants."

Slingsby also, unavoidably, made the acquaintance of fleas. In Norway's rural communities the blood-thirsty little pests were at that time looked upon as an evil to be suffered – no stigma of uncleanliness was attached to them, while harbouring lice was considered to be a shame. The history of the flea in Norway has been given in capsule form as follows: "People were much bothered with fleas in the olden days. Those insects nestled in the hay used in the beds and in animal skins used for bedclothes; when people began to use matresses, they disappeared." The early tourists definitely arrived at the seters prior to the time of matresses. And Slingsby gives this description of his strategy of self-defence: "I learned for the first time the real value of a good Scotch plaid and that it was a most useful adjunct to a sæter bed. Without a plaid one must keep all one's clothes on, excepting boots and coat. With a plaid one can take most of them off, can wrap one's feet well and leave a good length for the head, then roll up almost like a Chrysalis and fasten the fold securely with safety pins, and after drawing over oneself the skins and saying to one's companions, "God nat" (Good night), can boldly defy the attacks of the evil creatures."

The lodges built by DNT were, it is presumed, devoid of fleas. But luxurious those early lodges were not. Here is Hubert Smith's description of the first one, Tvinnehaugen: "The chalet consists of two rooms, with superiour kind of "bunks", or bedsteads, but no fittings of any kind. The windows are too low to obtain a pleasant view of the lake when standing up, and are not adapted for ventilation. There is a stove in one room. . . . It is a shelter from the storm,

Groping through the mists.

"Skarvdalseggen and Raudalstind from Urdadalen" is the caption of this picture. It dates from the period, the 1880's, when winter tourists for the first time skied through Jotunheimen from north to south – by way of that very valley. Photo by Axel Lindahl.

wind and night-air, and is not intended for anything more." This was, however, before Gudbrand Skattebu became the host of Tvinnehaugen, and set about enlarging the place and making it more cozy. And within 20 years DNT had four lodges and two small cottages in Jotunheimen, plus Vinje's house at Eidsbu, bought by Thomas Heftye after the author's death, and open to tourists. Furthermore, by offering economic aid the association had encouraged the building of four private lodges.

The third task to be tackled, was that of making hiking in the area safe for the average tourist. In its earliest years DNT concentrated on locating guides who could be licenced, and on establishing fair guiding fees. Then map-making came into focus, as did the marking of trails and building of foot-bridges; the latter two subject are covered by another article, written by Claus Helberg, through many years a mainstay of DNT.

Jotunheimen now has a fully built-out network of trails and lodges. And anybody wanting further information can get it through DNT. Incidentally, to fully appreciate the work done by that association, one has to realize that during its first decades members were few, making up in enthusiasm for what they lacked in numbers – even at the association's 50th anniversary in the year 1918, membership had barely nudged above 5000.

Braving the Winter Storms

The first tourist to brave Jotunheimen in winter was none other than that Englishman who has already been mentioned a number of times in this book, and who has become a legend to Norwegian mountaineers: William Cecil Slingsby. With the guide Torgeir Sulheim of Fortun, by then his friend, and a Halvar Halvarsen, evidently also of that community, he skied from Helgedalen through the Keisaren pass to Guridalen seter (in the process learning how to ski). They continued through the snow on foot to Vormeli, where they spent some time unsuccessfully bear hunting. Then they made their way down Utladalen to Vetti, where they arrived as the first winter visitors to that place. The time was November of the year 1880. And when trying to describe the view east from Keisaren, with "shimmering snow-fields" and "dark precipices which . . . can never hold snow, they can only be peppered as it were", Slingsby seems, for once, to be almost at a loss for words – he ends thus: "I wish that each one of my readers could, at least once in life, see such a scene as this, for, if he saw no other of a similar nature, this one would be sufficient to awaken in him, if need be, and to foster a love of mountain scenery which could only be terminated at his death."

Possibly inspired by Slingsby's venture, Thomas Heftye, youngest son of

From Sikkilsdalen.

DNT's first president, decided to ski through Jotunheimen from Bøverdalen to Eidsbu at Christmas time of the year 1886. He set out accompanied by a friend, and with Ola Røysheim and Knut Vole as guides. An attempt at making a first winter ascent of Galdhøpiggen was given up when Heftye got serious trouble with a knee. But even when his knee became badly swollen, he refused to abandon the whole project; they reached Gjendebu and made a sidetrip from there to Eidsbu, the two tourists then returning to the capital. The next Christmas Day found Heftye and Vole at the top of Galdhøpiggen; Vole also was guide to the first party ascending Glittertind in winter.

But only a few adventurous people followed suit; not until the turn of the century did winter tourism in Jotunheimen begin to gain momentum. And a bit of prodding by the Ski Association was needed to make the owners of Glitterheim open that lodge for ski tourists at Easter of the year 1907. The experiment was a success, and since then Easter traffic in Jotunheimen has increased steadily – one by one DNT's lodges, as well as those privately

Langvatnet towards Visbretind.

Besshø with Bessvatn in the foreground. Bessvatn is within fairly easy walking distance (some 3 km, 425 m to climb) from Bessheim, on rt. 51 by Øvre Sjodalsvatn.

owned, have opened for business at that time of the year. During later years some of the lodges have even expanded their winter season. – But anybody wanting further information is again referred to that splendid institution, Den Norske Turistforening.

A Paradox: Jotunheimen by Car

The best way to travel in Jotunheimen is on foot. The next best way is also travelling on foot. But since a number of people for valid reasons are unable to do that, I shall admit that it is possible to see quite a bit of those mountains with a minimum of walking – at least between the middle of June and October, when the mountain roads are kept open. For Jotunheimen now is closely encircled by roads; a few even penetrate deeply into the area.

A good road map may be bought in any bookshop, and the route runs as follows (arbitrarily starting from Turtagrø and going south): The toll road from Turtagrø to Øvre Årdal; rt. 53 Ø.Årdal – Hugostua; E 68 Hugostua –

Below: In a lemming year this curious little character may be met everywhere in Jotunheimen.

Next page: From Griningsdalen. An unmarked road a little more than a kilometer north of Nedre Sjodalsvatn leads to Griningsdalen and to Kampen seter.

Hemsing bru; follow signs to and take the toll road across Slettefjell to Beitostølen; rt. 51 Beitostølen – Randen; rt. 15 Randen – Lom; rt. 55 Lom – Turtagrø. The distance is a little more than 300 km and easily covered in a day, even though the roads are of varying standard. But I strongly advise against that kind of hurry. Taking one's time and making a number of the side-trips indicated by the map (almost all are worth-while) will be much more interesting. And the area has overnight accommodations to please most tastes and purses. One warning, though: The parts of Jotunheimen approachable by car are generally the ones developed for hydroelectric power purposes – expect to see dry riverbeds, dams, power lines and big heaps of rock debris.

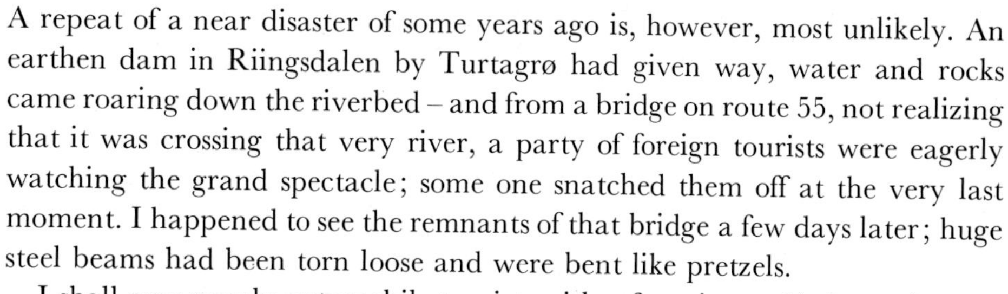

A repeat of a near disaster of some years ago is, however, most unlikely. An earthen dam in Riingsdalen by Turtagrø had given way, water and rocks came roaring down the riverbed – and from a bridge on route 55, not realizing that it was crossing that very river, a party of foreign tourists were eagerly watching the grand spectacle; some one snatched them off at the very last moment. I happened to see the remnants of that bridge a few days later; huge steel beams had been torn loose and were bent like pretzels.

I shall now supply automobile tourists with a few pieces of information not given elsewhere in this book – and I shall follow the example of some old-time guides in shifting between fact and legend. But I shall *not* give a blow-by-blow tour pointing out that here or there that lake or mountain comes into view – the kind of people I have in mind, would have much more fun stopping their car, looking at the map and finding out for themselves.

If approaching on rt. 55 along Sognefjord, one enters Jotunheimen proper as that road, having left the fjord behind, turns north, towards the community of Fortun. And as sentinels, high above the valley, one on each side of the steep Berdalen, lie the farms Furås and Fuglesteg. They sit on shelves in the side of the valley, and one practically has to break one's neck to see them. The story just *may* be true that at one of Fortun's "shelf farms" people never paid their taxes – when the sheriff approached, they merely pulled up the ladder that offered the only access to the place. The side-trip up Fortunsdalen to Nørdstedalsseter, DNT lodge, is dramatic in places, and is not recommended to people who easily get dizzy, or who would rather avoid driving on a narrow road (reversing and manoeuvering may be necessary if meeting another car) along a precipice. By the way, Fortunsdalen is just as prone to rock-slides as it seems. A friend of mine who grew up there, says that he just accepted the danger as a part of life, and never thought much of it – until he had moved away and came back some years later. Other districts prone to avalanches and to rock- or earthslides are Årdal and Lom.

There was, however, a time when people of Årdal hoped that their mountains had more to offer than slides. Around the year 1700 copper was found west of Fardalen (on the route Turtagrø – Ø.Årdal) – later silver, and even gold. A number of mine shafts were dug and ore brought out; a whole community centered on mining grew up by Årdalsvatnet. But getting that

View from Storebjørn, tallest of Smørstabbtindene. In the foreground Sjurtungstind, to the right Raudalstindene. Then, further in the background, Mjølkedalstind and Sjogholstind flanking the lower Olavsbunuten (named for DNT's cottage Olavsbu). To the left Raudalseggi. A toll road taking off from rt. 55 runs south through Leirdalen to Leirvassbu lodge, passing Storebjørn on the way – it cuts deeply in towards the area shown in the picture. As far as scenery is concerned, it offers nothing but rugged barreness: jagged peaks, glaciers, rushing mountain streams –.

copper out was hard work, the main shaft is located at an altitude of 1500 m and fully 10 km as the crow flies from Farnes, out of where the ore was shipped. And estimates proved to have been too optimistic; activities terminated in the 1760's. However, the whole area around Fardalen is dotted with relics of mining: remnants of roads, foundations of houses, mine shafts.

And talking of the past – anybody interested in archeology would want to know that Årdal has a rare relic of the Viking Age. At Ytre Moa, not far from the junction of Tya and Utla, a farm from that period has been excavated. The place evidently was abandoned during the 10th century, which is the reason for the find; most farms of that period remained in use into the Middle Ages, and remnants of Viking Age houses were destroyed.

Tyin's connection with the distant past has been mentioned often enough in this book – I shall supply a story of more recent times, that of a near shipwreck at an altitude of 1000 m plus. It happened in the autumn of the year 1915, when M/B Jotunheim, at that time trafficking Tyin, made its last trip of the year from Tyinholmen. Winds were blowing at severe gale force, and the boat, heavily loaded, was pulling two rowboats with live pigs in crates. Soon the rowboats were getting swamped and were in danger of sinking, dragging "Jotunheim" down with them. Some brave man broke the crates, giving the pigs a chance to swim for their lives, before those rowboats were set adrift. "Jotunheim" found a port of refuge by Breikvam, and people

Reindeer bucks by Bukkeholstind. Bukkeholstind is one of the many sights to be behold on Jotunheimen's easiest trail, that between the lodges Spiterstulen (Visdalen) and Leirvassbu (Leirdalen). That trail (no very strenuous climbs, and even easier from Leirvassbu to Spiterstulen than vice versa) is marked on tourist maps as a 4-5 hour hike. A toll road through Visdalen to Spiterstulen takes off from rt. 55 in Bøverdalen by the old tourist inn Røisheim, and though less spectacular than the Leirdalen route, is most worth-while. From Spiterstulen a fairly easy and guided hike offers a tour of a glacier cataract (Svellnosbreen).

went ashore for the night. But full alarm was given when the boat did not arrive at its destination – a state of high drama was approached when the empty boats and the pigs, live and drowned, were found – . Now scheduled boat service on Tyin is a thing of the past, and the road along the lake's eastern shore goes all the way to Eidsbugarden, named for Vinje's cottage, still there.

From Hugostua going west on E 68 to Kyrkjestølene and the site of the medieval church of St. Thomas, is a relatively short detour recommended for people with a lively imagination. Of the church and the fair nothing is left except a building site, a few of the fittings of that church found in a new one raised nearby, and a stone house. And while in the process of conjuring up the past, one might as well also go back all the way to the Stone Age. Some 8500 years ago skin-clad hunters roamed that very area.

But the church of St. Thomas was what is known as a stave church, which in essence means a wooden church where a system of posts and girders, and not the walls, is the carrying element. And anybody interested in architecture or history of art should have an excellent opportunity of studying medieval stave churches at a Jotunheimen-by-car-tour. Six such churches are passed en route or reached by fairly easy detours: Borgund (on E 68 in Lærdal), Øye (on E 68, and rather loosely reconstructed from materials stored under a later church), Høre (Hurum) and Lomen, both in Vestre Slidre, Hegge (in Øystre

Slidre), Lom (at the junction of routes 15 and 55). Those churches vary in use of the basic system of construction, and all have interesting details architecturally as well as decoration-wise, but to the average tourist one or two should suffice. Of interest pertaining to the architecture and history of the area are also the museums of Fagernes in Valdres (which even includes a mock-up of reindeer pitfalls and archers' hideouts) and Lom.

Scheduled motorboats still run on Bygdin and Gjende, covering areas that can not be reached by car. But the Bygdin boat ran into trouble this year: It had been taken ashore to be enlarged, and by the time is was ready for re-launching, Bygdin, used for hydroelectric power, had been tapped down so far that launching was temporarily impossible. And at Gjendebu is still found the "romantic" stone seter house where Gjendine Slålien was born. However, to tourists of the early 1870's it hardly seemed romantic, quarters were too cramped. One man complains that the cows were milked in his bedroom at dawn; another tells of sleeping on the floor, a fate he shared with a couple of drovers – the three woke up huddled together by the wall, having instinctively sought to each other for warmth in the chilly night.

But from the 1870's and onwards, a popular tourist's centre was found at Bessun seter by Øvre Sjodalsvatn. There Peter Tronhus, one of Jo Gjende's hunting pals, presided as host. And Peter was a famed teller of yarns and player of the fiddle, while his wife, Kari, struggled to care for the material needs of their guests. Under his roof gathered foreigners, local people and people from the towns, finding an atmosphere with which the nearby DNT lodge could not compete – a flickering light from the fireplace made faces blush, while Peter entertained with music and fantastic tales.

And while in a romantic mood – further down Sjodalen (signs by rt. 51 show where to take off from the main road) is Ridderspranget, a wild, narrow canyon through which the river Sjoa, violently protesting, is forced. According to a legend (not confirmed) a nobleman of medieval times, with his abducted bride, escaped his pursuers by making his horse jump across that canyon – then demonstrated by example that he would push into the boiling inferno below anyone who tried to follow. Unconfirmed is also a story from a seter across the river: a boy, staying there alone, was tempted by a beautiful hulder and saved himself from sin by shooting at her. And equally unconfirmed is the story of a boy at Randsverk, who chose another way out of the same dilemma: he married the hulder girl and got riches as her dowry.

From Randsverk it is possible to make a toll road detour by way of Tesse, ending up at Randen or Garmo. The side trip into Veodalen requires a lot from the driver – the road is awful – , but offers Jotunheimen's best view of the majestic Glittertind; also, in the shade of Heranoshø, the possibility of seeing reindeer pitfalls "in the field". And to any one who prefers a grand panorama, a detour via Vågå to the top of Blåhø is recommended – a large part of Southern Norway may be seen from that vantage point.

The view is even grander from Galdhøpiggen, but there the road goes part way only, from Galde in Bøverdalen to Juvasshytta. The climb from Juvasshytta to the top, some 600 m, is, however, not considered very strenuous.

And then, on Sognefjell, a few mementos of the past are found within a stone's throw from the road. There is Fantesteinen, "the bad-guy boulder", (marked with a sign) behind which robbers are supposed to have lain in ambush. And about half-way between Krossbu and Turtagrø, where a side-road takes off to the north, are a cluster of cairns. Here, according to tradition, six men from Lom died in a blizzard in the year 1813 – but the six cairns raised in memory of them, have been supplemented by a veritable cairn forest; tourists, not knowing the story, have felt encouraged to build their own. Further on, just before the road crosses a dam at the outlet of Hervatnet, a stone hut sits between the road and the lake – supposedly the very one in which Henrik Ibsen was marooned by bad weather.

Finally, as the road dives towards Turtagrø and Fortun, there is that famous view of Hurrungane. I believe it was a citizen of gentle Denmark who commented that the place looked as if the Lord forgot to tidy up when He had finished creating – .

Besseggen between Bessvatn and Gjende. Getting to this lofty perch involves a hike of some 5 km and a climb of 760 m from Gjendesheim (reached by car from rt. 51). And for anybody who is at all able to do this, it is certainly worth it!

Literary Review a Century Later

Among British literature on Scandinavia two pieces seem to survive the onslaught of time: a certain Mr. Shakespeare's play concerning a morbid Dane, Hamlet, and "THREE IN NORWAY BY TWO OF THEM" – . Within another context, the world of Norwegian mountaineering, the three, "the Skipper", "Esau" and "John", are just about as well-known as their compatriot William Cecil Slingsby.

The "three" spent a summer and autumn of the early 1880's hunting and fishing in the Gjende area. "The Skipper" had been to Norway before – hence the name –, and they had planned their trip in detail, bringing along Canadian canoes. Jens Trondhus, a son of Peter, was their favourite guide; they were unhappy that they could not secure his services very often. But like many others, they greatly enjoyed their visits to Bessun seter.

A certain feeling of awe is inescapable as I study the photograph of an oven, supposedly the very one constructed by the famous trio from rough stones at their Gjende campsite, near the mouth of Memuruelven. If the "two of them" are to be trusted (and they insist they are recounting the "simple facts, but that here and there is introduced some slight fiction which is too obvious to require any comment"), a great many delicacies have been baked in that primitive oven: bread, rolls, biscuits, wimberry tarts – and, not to forget, mouthwatering venison pies. It is truly a pity that I have not noticed the oven on my previous visits to the site!

Yet I can vividly imagine the three, a memorable August evening approximately a hundred years ago, when they were in the process of producing a pie to outdo all other pies: "It was made in our largest baking tin, 12 inches across, and contained nearly a hind quarter of venison, our last six eggs, a heart, a liver, and about 1 1/2 lb. of bacon. The crust was put on about nine o'clock. And after we had all gazed at it and unanimously agreed that it was the "boss pie", we bore it proudly but gingerly to the oven, heated by John seven times hotter than before, and now gaping to receive it; a great full moon rose from behind the mountains and seemed to smile on our good work; the

The oven by Memurubu, memento of "Three in Norway by two of them".

"The camp in Memurudalen".

Below: Disgusted with life (the Skipper). Both drawings are from the book.

bright fire shed a glow over the three figures bending o'er the simmering treasure, and a more peaceful, domestic group it would be impossible to conceive. About eleven John and the Skipper turned in, but outside could be seen for some time the solitary form of Esau still crouching over the expiring embers of the oven, and tending with a mother's care the tempting food that he already tasted in imagination."

But what do we know about the background of these men of fame? It is only fair to respect their wish for anonymity – they did, however, obviously belong to a group of adventurous Britons who possessed the time and means to travel. And they show a rather unpleasant arrogance towards "the natives", in this context meaning the inhabitants of Norway. This patronizing attitude would, in fact, have been close to unbearable, were it not compensated for by their disarming willingness poke fun at themselves: "Foreigners have a curious prejudice which leads them to adopt different systems of coinage and measurement from those in favour in England. But shall a Briton pander to this prejudice by making any use of their ridiculous figures. Decidedly not!"

They also seem to have been fascinated by Jotunheimen, much as are the tourists, "native" or foreign, of our day. They write: "Oh blessed Norway! when we get back to the turmoil, troubles and pleasures of a London season how shall we long for you! There is only one word to describe this existence, and that is Freedom – freedom from care, freedom from resistance, and from the struggle for life." Nostalgically they wish to turn time back "a hundred generations", to retrograde into man's "primeval condition". And so, in certain ways, they actually do. There is, however, a remarkable contrast between their seeming bloodthirstiness – they consider it a right and a duty to shoot practically anything that flies, or moves on four feet –, and their library of "light literature", consisting of Shakespeare, Longfellow, Dr. Johnson's Table-talk etc. Yet – we, of the twentieth century, ought not to be surprised; we should know that civilization is less than skin deep.

By boat on Gjende in the 1970's. Marie Hoft, in charge of DNT's Gjendebu lodge for 35 years (1938-72).

But why has the description, given by these three rogues of their hunting and fishing adventures, endeared them to so many Norwegian readers? Their cut-to-the-bone, yet marvellously satisfying descriptions of scenery, sunsets, moonlight, answers the question in part only. The main reason is their wit and irrepressible high spirits. And they seem to know by unerring instinct how to tell a story; they know exactly where to exaggerate shamelessly and where to stop short and leave the rest to the reader's imagination. Also, their style, mock serious, is priceless. Unfortunately, one sample will have to suffice: The description of a confrontation between the Skipper and Ola, guide to the trio and an incorrigible dawdler. This time Ola has commited the unforgivable sin of not showing up at the appointed time for reindeerstalking; the Skipper paddles angrily towards the eastern end of Gjende, looking for the culprit, "primed to exploding point by his two friends before starting, and as he had now paddled five miles from home without meeting the adversary, he was, to put it mildly, "indignant". So when he found Ola smoking serenely, and sculling along as though his brief span were going to stretch through the unending cycles of eternity, he gave way to the most horrible outbreak of temper in English, which must have lasted four or five minutes, and then -- he turned and left that hardy Norseman openmouthed and bewildered, looking as though he had seen the Strömkarl, or had had an interview with his mother-in-law." But the Skipper returned to camp "in the most beatific frame of mind; the relief of the storm of temper and bad language had been so great to him, that he was filled with blessed joy. He said it was the most invigorating and refreshing pastime he ever indulged in, for Ola could not understand a word of it, and therefore no remorse could follow the outburst".

But I have just mentioned sampling – and we left the "boss pie" simmering in the oven. Let me hasten to assure the reader that this splendid work of art fulfilled all expectations.

The fate of the oven is, however, less certain. For as the trio was breaking camp, "Esau's last act was to fill two brass cartridge cases with water and hammer them firmly into each other; the air-tight boiler so formed he put into the fire under the oven, and after waiting a short time for the explosion, forgot all about it and went away without telling any one. Just then John arrived at the spot to see if there were any loose belongings lying about, and was horrified to observe the oven suddenly elevate itself into the air and disappearing among the clouds with a loud report."

So, returning to that photo of the oven: Either it is a case of mistaken identity – or could, possibly, the vivid description of the oven's dramatic end have been embellished with "some slight fiction" – ?

By Gjendeosen, the eastern end of that lake.

The Summits — and Beyond

The more readily accessible mountains of Jotunheimen almost certainly had been climbed long before the "first ascents" recorded in modern times. It is true that as a rule people of old were not alpinists – though there seems to have been exceptions. But the huntsmen followed their prey, and where the reindeer climbed to the top, so did their pursuers. Now, deer have been observed and even photographed, at the top of Fannaråken. Furthermore, Hubert Smith reports from his Galdhøpiggen ascent that "On the hanging precipice of rocks, the highest in Norway, a reindeer had met its death." And an

On top of Gjertvasstind – Emanuel Mohn's «special» peak.

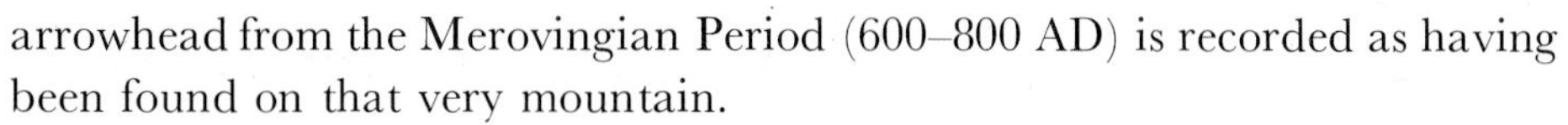

arrowhead from the Merovingian Period (600–800 AD) is recorded as having been found on that very mountain.

But not only the "first ascents" of easily climbed peaks may be doubtful as such. There is the case of Mellomste Skagastølstind, the first ascent of which is credited to the Dane Carl Hall and his guide Mathias Soggemoen in the year 1884. Going back 62 years, to 1822, one finds this report by N. M. Blytt from his visit to Fortun and Turtagrø that year:" One of the party asked the owner of Skagastølen if it was difficult to climb the lowest of Skagastølstindene. 'One can ride a horse to the top,' he replied, 'but the other high peaks are practically unclimbable.' Still, his grandfather once had taken courage and climbed the middle one, and had happily reached the summit. . . (then) he became frightened and wanted to go down in a hurry. But it seemed impossible to locate the cracks where he had found support for hands and feet on the way up. He feared for his life, and in his distress promised to give a cow to the poor if he came down alive, which he did. But since that time the farmers have seen it as a presumption to even think of climbing one of those peaks." So far Blytt.

The Norwegian historian A. O. Øverland bemoans (in the year 1904) the fact that Keilhau left no report of his and Boeck's recorded "first ascent" of Nordre Skagastølstind. Maybe the answer is given above: Keilhau knew that they were not first on that summit, and, furthermore, the climb was so easy that not even Keilhau could make it dramatic.

The same may well have been the case with Gottfred Bohr, who is credited with the first ascent of Nordre Dyrhaugstind (Hurrungane) on July 5th of the year 1820, a few weeks prior to Boeck's and Keilhau's venture on Nordre Skagastølstind. Bohr refers to his feat only in a footnote to the account of his ascent of Lodalskåpa (Jostedalsbreen), mentioning that he has calculated the height of Store Skagastølstind from Dyrhaugstind.

That fairly recent ascents also might be overlooked, is shown by a second "first ascent" of Glittertind accomplished August 27th 1870, and duly reported in the British Alpine Journal of February the following year. The British conquerors of that peak may, however, have felt they had a right to disregard Wergeland's and Sletten's ascent 28 years earlier – which, again, most likely had been preceded by huntsmen's ascents – . Sir Martin Conway of The Alpine Club states that "an unrecorded ascent does not count"; to him recorded meant reported in climbing journals, and the 1852 ascent certainly was not.

What, then, is to be considered a "first ascent"? That, apparently, is a matter of definition. Which does not in the least detract from the achievement of the alpinists who "conquered" Jotunheimen.

The Classic Period

As should properly be the case with periods, the classic one of alpinism in Norway can be divided into "early", "high" and "late".

The early classic comprises the period of the 1870's and a story of three men of quite different personalities.

Emanuel Mohn (1842–91) was a student from the city of Bergen, and had been greatly influenced by the mountain-romanticism of Vinje and his circle. His first personal encounter with Jotunheimen was a hike through the area in the year 1868; he returned the following year. And Jotunheimen became his

passion. Mohn was a through-and-through enthusiast who felt compelled to share his excitement with others. And though his style was on the bombastic side, it was in pact with the taste of the times and caught on. In line with DNT's work he also gave detailed descriptions of routes and even drew sketches. His climbing ventures began in the year 1874 with the ascent of three peaks, none of which were in the alpine category: Dyrhaugstind, Glittertind and Nautgardstind (Glittertind's neighbour to the east). And, incidentally, we get a third «first» on Glittertind; Mohn has been hailed as the first *Norwegian tourist* (no less) to attain the summit of that peak. Yet he managed to make Norwegian mountaineering history that year – it was the year when he first met the British alpinist William Cecil Slingsby.

Slingsby (1849–1929), a man who during some 40 years as an active climber was to make many difficult ascents in various countries, was born a generation too late to take part in the great assault on the Alps; when he came of age, all the principal summits of that range had been scaled. He came to Norway for the first time in the year 1872 – and discovered a multitude of unclimbed peaks. That year he was also confronted with the mountain which became an obsession with him: Store Skagastølstind. Years later he wrote: "I shall never forget as long as I live my first view of Skagastølstind, the grandest European mountain north of the Alps." The following summer he was detained in England with a badly sprained ancle. But the year after he came back and partook in what he terms "the first glacier pass crossing in the Horungtinder" (through Riingskaret) – a statement that is doubtful in view of pastor Bøyesen's report, half a century earlier, of local people travelling between Årdal and Fortun through Hurrungane, using ropes on the glaciers. He also scaled his first maiden peak, one of Urda(Ula)dalstindene. He returned to Norway in the year 1875, that time bringing his sister – and we get a fourth "first" on Glittertind; on July 30th at 5 PM she "stepped on the top of this peerless white dome, and completed the first ascent by a lady of the second highest mountain in Scandinavia".

The tour that was to bring Mohn and Slingsby each to the summit of the peak of his heart's desire, took place the year following, after being thoroughly planned in an exchange of letters. They had secured as a guide Knut Lykken of Øystre Slidre, a reindeer hunter well-known as a mountain guide. The trio "warmed up" on a few mountains around Bygdin, of which Torfinnstind was Mohn's first maiden peak. "His enthusiasm was unbounded," Slingby reports. "Never before or since have I seen any man in such raptures with the beauty of Nature." Then, making a first ascent of Uranostind on the way, they proceeded to Skogadalsbøen and were in position for an assault on Hurrungane. Mohn's favourite, Gjertvasstind (then known as Østre Styggedalstind) proved to be no problem. Store Skagastølstind was, however, an entirely different story. They reached the skar (col) between Vesle and Store Skagastølstind, some 150 m below the summit of Store, late in the afternoon of July 21st. And even Slingsby feared that tower there facing them, springing "from the glacier which we had ascended, nearly perpendicular and almost entirely without ledges" might prove too formidable. The following exchange, a classic in Norwegian mountaineering history, took place: "What do you think of it, Mohn?" "Well, I suppose that we now can say it is perfectly impossible." "We have not yet proven it to be so; we must not give it up without a try. Will you come?" "No." "Knut, will you?" "No, I shall not risk my life there." "I will at least try, though I do not think I can manage it."

And try Slingsby did, though, in his own words, "suffice it to say that what

Store Skagastølstind veiled by the mists of morning. The picture is taken from "Mohn's skar" early in July, and the climbers are following Slingsby's first ascent route to the summit.

Styggedalsbreen with Styggedalstindene. Gjertvasskar and Gjertvasstind to the left.

under the most favourable conditions must be a tough piece of work, was made more so by the films of ice with which every little ledge was veneered". Yet he kept struggling on. When the goal practically seemed within reach, "there was a ridge – a knife-edged affair – perhaps sixty yards long. . . . There are three peaklets and a notch in the ridge which latter again almost stopped me. For the first time I had to trust an overhanging and rather loose rocky ledge. I tried it well, then hauled myself up to terra firma, and in a few strides, a little above half an hour after leaving my friends, I gained the unsullied crown of the peerless Skagastølstind." Slingsby's reaction was, however, not the wild enthusiasm that would have been Mohn's, but rather "a feeling of silent worship and reverence" – .

Slingsby returned to Norway many a time and made many an ascent here.

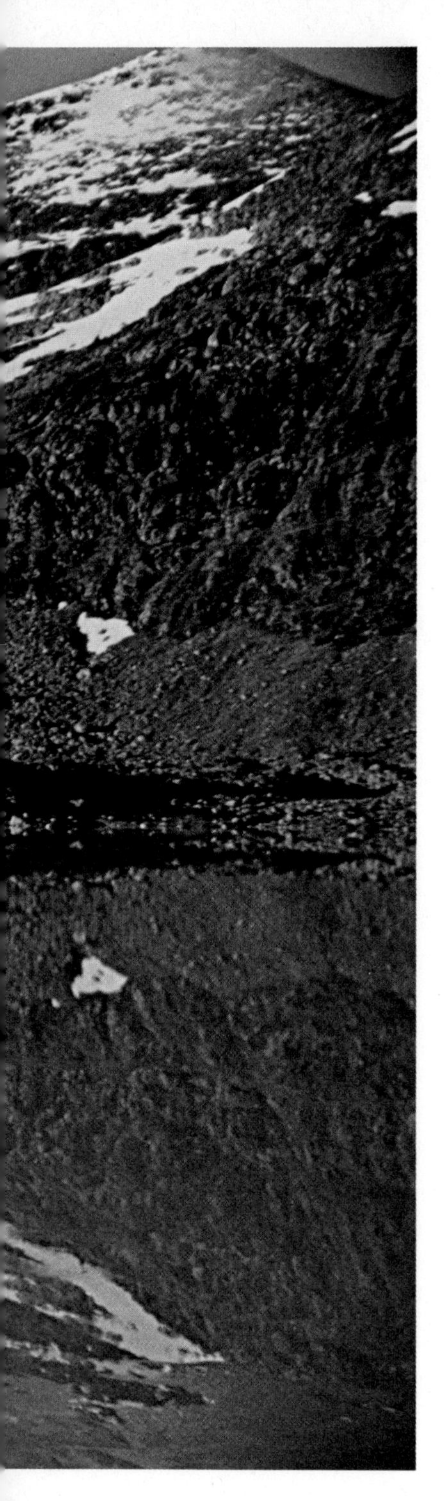

But Mohn followed a different course. The summer with Slingsby had taught him a great deal about climbing, and he had seen his own limitations. He spent two more summers mountaineering and exploring in Jotunheimen; then, somehow, he seems to have run out of enthusiasm. "I have become old among the peaks, I know them inside and out", he writes; "I seldom get overwhelmed any more." And "I long for the sheltered valley." One reason for his weariness may have been the derision he suffered for not having gone with Slingsby to the top of Skagastølstind. When he defended himself by saying that he doubted any Norwegian mountaineer would have been up to such a task, a young hot-head, Harald Petersen, rushed off to climb that peak. He made a vain attempt in the year 1877, but succeeded the following year – by luck alone saved from getting killed in the process.

Three more Norwegians, Johannes Heftye (son of DNT's president) and two guides from Årdal, Jens Klingenberg and Peder Melheim, reached the coveted summit in the year 1880. But Heftye, the third of the climbers mentioned above as being active in Jotunheimen's "early classic" period, seems to have been driven mostly by a wish to spite Slingsby, possibly a manifestation of misguided nationalistic pride. He even went to the length of writing a pamphlet with the main purpose of defaming the Englishman as a climber, and he insisted that his own conquest (with Knut Lykken) of Store Knutsholstind – between Gjende and Bygdin – was a greater feat than Slingsby's ascent of Skagastølstind. Slingsby, usually good-humoured, clearly was irked; he describes Heftye's venture on Skagastølstind as that of "a young tourist, assisted by two good rock-climbers from Årdal – who have told me all about the expedition – ". And that barb undoubtedly hit home; Heftye, who discovered a new route to the top, *had* needed assistance by his agile guides in a difficult spot. As to Knutsholstind, Slingsby's chance of proving *his* point came the following year. He and his guide Johannes Vigdal, "the Solvorn warrior" (from Solvorn by the Luster fjord), were planning a try at that peak from Knutsholet, an ascent never before made. But when one of the girls in charge at Gjendebu, Oline Marie Sylfestsdotter, wanted to come along, Slingsby delightedly complied. And instead of the Knutsholet ascent, they chose Heftye's easier route from Svartdalen. The climb was no challenge to Slingsby and Vigdal and offered few problems to Marie – who even had the disadvantage of climbing in her Sunday best, a variant on the theme of national costume. Thus, on August 30th "at 1.28 we reached the summit, raised a loud cheer, and put Marie on the top of the little cairn, and very bonny she looked in her picturesque costume."

This was, incidentally, not the only time Slingsby delighted in introducing a novice to mountaineering. His gests of encouragement, in later years, to young climbers were also many.

And Slingsby, as well as other early Jotunheimen alpinists, had to train his own guides. But this seems to have been a fairly easy task, which is not surprising taking into account pastor Bøyesen's words about the typical male parishioner of his Lærdal-Årdal parish: "Dizziness is unknown. . . . He may lose his footing as others do – though he seems to remain on his feet where others fall – and he gets killed like others do, but the only reasons for that are his unbelievable daring and the fact that he lacks wings." Celebrated guides were, in addition to Knut Lykken and Johannes Vigdal, Thorgeir Sulheim and, somewhat later, Ola Berge and Ole Øiene – the latter three were from Fortun; from the early 1890's onwards Berge and Øiene were hosts of the two hotels at Turtagrø. In addition to being famous for his daring as a climber,

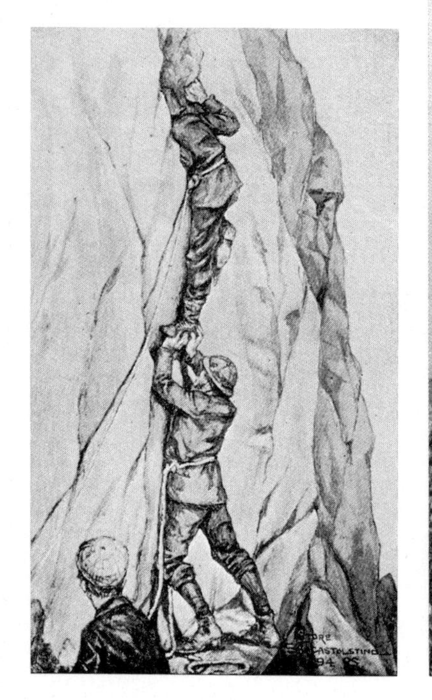

Above: Entering Heftye's chimney, the route Johannes Heftye discovered to the Top of Store Skagastølstind. Right: Therese Bertheau and Ola Berge at the top of "Storen", anchoring the rope for Slingsby, who is trying out a new route variant. Both pictures are from "The Northern Playground» by Slingsby, who comments on the climb pictured to the right: "It was a little over twenty years since I had the good luck to make the first ascent, and it was delightful now to be accompanied by Frøken Bertheau, who hade made in the year 1894 the first lady's ascent. She is a born mountaineer."

Vigdal was known for his bravery in assaulting the English language; some of his expressions became bywords with British alpinists, for instance "a bad mistake of the compass" meaning an error in judgement. And the independence typical of the Norwegian farmer marked them all. Sulheim once took Slingsby across the Utla river on horseback in a very rough spot – just to test his pluck. And Berge was known for his repartee. Once, when a rather stout tourist had been escorted – not to say transported – to the top of Store Skagastølstind ("Storen" for short) and safely brought back down, that gentleman remarked: "I didn't do too badly, really." "No – ," said Ola with a smile. "You didn't. But I might as well have hauled a piano to that summit.»"

Getting on to the "high classic" period, that decade was dominated by the Dane Carl Christian Hall (1848–1908). During the years 1882–90 he made 12 first ascents in Jotunheimen, 10 of them in Hurrungane, and on most accompanied by Mathias Soggemoen, a guide from Romsdal. Hall's style was more systematic than spectacular, and he has become known as the "scientist" among the Jotunheimen climbers. He attacked Hurrungane peak by peak, coming back one year after another. The last one, Østre Riingstind, was, however, figuratively snatched away from under his nose when the Englishman Arthur W. Andrews, climbing with J. Urdahl, scaled it in the year 1891.

And with that we have moved into "late classic", the period marked by traverses of Hurrungane's ridges. Hall was in on that, too, tackling the ridges piecemeal. And Slingsby was still around to partake in the fun. New in the elite group was Therese Bertheau, a woman who not only carried the torch

The classic picture of alpinists in Norway. Sitting on the front steps of Turtagrø hotel (from left to right): Wm. C. Slingsby, Howard Priestman, Therese Bertheau, an unknown British tourist. Standing: left Elias Hogrenning, mountaineer guide from Loen, right Ola Berge.

of Norwegian mountaineering around the turn of the century, but who had re-lit it after it sputtered out in the early 1880's. Her climbing exploits began in the year 1885 with an ascent of Uranostind – from that time on she single-mindedly worked at improving her skills, scaling peak after peak, until she stood on the top of "Storen" on July 29th 1894. She was the first woman there; by coincidence two other women scaled that peak on July 30th and 31st. In the year 1902 Therese Bertheau took part in an expedition traversing the entire northernmost ridge of Hurrungane, from Nordre Skagastølstind to Gjertvasstind; the guides were Ola Berge and Knut Fortun. The instigator of that venture, as well as a partaker in it, was Kristian Tandberg, a young Norwegian climber. He was the representative of a new generation, those who became the founders of Norsk Tindekubb (The Norwegian Alpine Club) in the year 1908. And with that began a new era.

Adventure or Competition

At the end of the classic period Jotunheimen climbing had arrived at that stage, reached in the Alps some 40 years previously, when the problem is finding new and more difficult routes on peaks already ascended – eventually of scaling those peaks in winter. Modern techniques with the use of pitons were introduced into the area in the 1930's by a later internationally known alpinist, Arne Næss. And they made possible ascents that had, till then, been beyond the dreams of even the most ambitious. In Hurrungane the final precipices to be tackled were those of Midtmaradalen, and the successful assaults took place in the late 1960's and early -70's. The degree of difficulty is indicated by the fact that the climbs of the eastern faces of Nordre and Søre Midtmaradalstind each took all of three days.

Now, with few new routes to conquer, to some climbers the main ambition has become that of making the various ascent faster than anybody has done it before them – .

And Jotunheimen has become Norway's teaching centre for mountaineering – people who would never have thought of climbing, join the courses because it is the thing to do. The Norwegian alpinist Per Vigerust has described some of the partakers (and graduates) thus: "We have 'The Salad' who is forever getting the rope tangled and keeps losing pitons and carabiners. 'The Lion' . . . is very forceful and attacks each and every obstacle with gusto, but may get hopelessly stuck in a chimney which a puny girl climbs with ease. To 'Wee Willie Winkie' the horror of mountaineering is concentrated in being let down by rope. He is a true hero, conquering undiluted fear each time he descends into the abyss. The instuctor's cry of 'straddle your legs' has no effect whatever; instead he closes his eyes (hence the name), Struggling to keep his balance. But the must difficult of pupils is 'The Grumbler'. What he will vividly remember from that course is endlessly waiting for his turn. However, maybe we meet him later on some peak where has set a new record, ascending its northern face in 3 hours and 27 minutes – or just home from the Himalayas..." Vigerust also mentions another kind of encounter: "Below a summit north of Gjende I once found a brand new nylon rope. Its original owner must have descended in great desperation, for the rope was fastened to – a belt, the former support of someone's trousers! Could 'The Salad' have left that rope thus? or possibly 'The Lion'?"

What, then, about the future of climbing in Jotunheimen? Are those mountains going to be reduced to a playground or a training area for people who go elsewhere to really test their skills? Is technique and the spirit of competition, the desire to be first or fastest, going to make Jotunheimen and, eventually, all the world's mountains obsolete victims of our "use-and-throw-away" society? John Hunt, the world famous alpinist, has, I believe, pointed out a better way:

"Mountains are the greatest handiwork of Nature. One of the reasons why we should enjoy climbing them is that they can correct our sense of proportion regarding ourselves; they can teach us a salutary lesson in humility. Herein lies the value of the past. For from the wisdom of experience it is possible to see clearly the importance of preserving the spirit of adventure in the future, yet of keeping that spirit free and objective, uncoloured by the prowess of individuals . . . and for any one person there is a whole life's adventure to visit and climb upon all the mountains of Europe alone – ."

Is a summit really sullied if someone else has built a cairn on it?

Bivouacking halfway up the precipice to the east of Austabottind. This was as high as the climbers came, they had to descend because of adverse weather.

Trailmarking to a" T"

Claus Helberg

Of Cairns and Paint

"You spoil the view with that red paint!" was the encouraging welcome I received at "hytta på bandet", "the cottage in the notch" by Store Skagastølstind. And that was after a strenuous hike up Midtmaradalen lugging a heavy rucksack, a painter's brush and a pail full of paint – not the easiest things to carry, really, when one needs both hands to hang on to sheer cliffs. "People ought to use maps," my climber friend went on. "Anyone who can't find his way up here without the aid of your red T's, had better choose an easier route – for the sake of his own health." Upon which he left for a refreshing evening ascent of Store Skagastølstind.

I threw a glance at him as he was happily climbing that rugged peak, unmarred by annoying red T's of the kind I had been giving a fresh coat of paint on my way up.

Could he, just possibly, be right? Might the Norwegian Tourist Association (DNT) as well cease building cairns and painting T's to mark the trails, leave alone the mountain areas still untouched, and let hikers choose their own paths? Certainly a great deal of public sentiment goes against encroachment upon the patches of wilderness left, even including DNT's activity of marking new trails and maintaining old ones.

However, DNT did not invent cairns.

From time immemorial those have been used to mark trails and boundaries, and as seamarks and landmarks. Some have been painstakingly constructed, others more casually erected, and some consist of one stone only, easily recognizable by its shape or colour. Cairns are also found on the summits of high peaks, and many of those have been built as aids to map-making. Others have been erected to commemorate first ascents or traverses. And herders have built many, most for no apparent reason. Then there are rows of small cairns leading nowhere – and probably showing the way to some huntsman's long forgotten storage place for meat.

But when DNT began its trail-marking activity in Jotunheimen, more than a hundred years ago, only a few cairn-marked trails existed: the old trails across Sognefjellet and Valdresflya, the trail through Leirdalen and Storådalen to the seters by Gjende, and the trail from Turtagrø through the Keisaren pass to the seters in Guridalen and Utladalen. And maps were non-existent or unreliable.

A few courageous hikers made it on their own, but most used guides until DNT began its work of marking trails. One of the important tasks of that association during its first years was registering guides, coming to agreement upon fair charges and seeing to it that they were complied with. However, to most people hiring guides was impractical as well as too expensive – and it seemed more interesting to find one's own way. In the DNT Yearbook of 1871 a British member, W. R. Thelwall, suggested that the association use a special, easily recognizable, type of cairn, so that tourists would not be led astray by all kinds of different ones; he even submitted a design. The association adopted Thelwall's idea, and the first of the new cairn-marked trails was ready in the year 1874: the route from Bessheim to Memurubu by way of Besseggen. Thousands of "Thelwall's cairns" now mark Norwegian mountain trails – though few people are aware of their origin.

Yet, on a rock-strewn slope hikers may have trouble locating even a characteristic cairn.

And in the year 1880 someone hit upon the idea of painting an emblem at the top of each cairn; the red T thus has been used for almost a century. The association's Annual Report of 1883 mentions that Gudbrand Skattebu, the huntsman and guide, had been marking the trail from Tyin towards Vetti, as far as Smoget, with cairns and red T's; the expense for paint was kr. 4. And that paint was durable, his T's still show perfectly well, as does the year 1883 painted on one of the stones.

Most of Jotunheimen's trails, once marked, demand little in the way of maintenance. The T's may become weatherbeaten and pale. But tens of thousands of hikers' feet keep wearing those trails down until it is practically

DNT's "cottage in the notch" with the view of Midtmaradalen.

A British member of DNT, W. B. Thelwall Esq., wrote in the Assiociation's Yearbook of 1871: "I would suggest that the Club should adapt a peculiar and uniform mark of its own, say a cairn of 3 or 4 stones placed a little apart with one on the top so that the light can be seen through them..."

impossible to get lost – and across patches of snow the tracks are clear and easy to follow, footbridges cross the streams, at crossroads guideposts show the way.

One hardly needs be an expert map reader to make the rounds from one lodge or cottage to another in Jotunheimen these days.

However, the area also has difficult routes, trails traversing or climbing precarious precipices or crossing glaciers. There are trails to suit the veteran as well as the novice, and people who need a guide on the glaciers, which means everyone without plenty experience and know-how, can get one.

My climber friend has descended from the heights; we are enjoying the summer evening and the spectacular view of Midtmaradalen. Far below us the winding river looks like a silver ribbon casually discarded on the lush green carpet of the valley floor – on both sides framed by mighty peaks.

One T-marked trail leads from here down the precipices to the bottom of that valley, then climbs steeply up to the Midtmaradalen ridge and from there goes into Stølsmaradalen, an out-of-the-way place where two seters were in use until the mid-1930's. DNT has now restored the seter houses, and they make very pleasant lodgings for hikers; as part of the project the Årdal Tourist Association has cairn-marked the old road from Fardalen to Stølsmaradalen, And this was done in the nick of time: the houses were on the verge of collapsing, and the road, running some 20 km through rugged terrain, reaching an altitude of 1200 m and for a stretch following the timberline to the west of Utladalen, was in the process of becoming overgrown. Another old, interesting and spectacular trail leads from Stølsmaradalen down the extremely steep Brennteigen to Vetti. Map and compass are of no use there; anyone losing his way would be lucky indeed to make it to Vetti without breaking his neck. And without those red T's, it is doubtful whether anybody nowadays would experience the wild beauty of Stølsmaradalen. Rediscovering, marking and maintaining seter roads of this kind is a means of preserving part of our cultural heritage – .

Even my climber friend nods in agreement.

Of Snow and Sticks

In winter another kind of trailmarkers are used: sticks, each one at least 1.50 m long.

The main season for cross-country skiing in the Norwegian mountains is Easter; many people take part of their vacation at that time. In Jotunheimen the lodges and cottages are prepared to receive hordes of skiers, and all the main trails have to be marked.

We start out from Krossbu Thursday before Palm Sunday – three men together, each carrying three big bundles of sticks, 50 to the bunch. Our task is that of marking the trail towards Nørdstedalseter (in Fortunsdalen), and we shall keep at that job as long as we have sticks. My two companions will then return to Krossbu, while I go on to Nørdstedalseter.

At 20 m intervals we secure sticks in the snow. And our burdens, heavy and cumbersome as we climb Krosshø, gradually lighten. On the steep descent towards Storevatn we put the markers closer together, and across the lake they are supposed to form a straight line – which makes it necessary to aim carefully for a group of boulders on the opposite shore. Marking a trail, one is responsible for the ones who are to follow. And, anyhow, leaving a straight track is a matter of pride.

By Liabrevatnet, en route Krossbu – Nørdstedalsseter.

Near the western shore of that lake we have used up our sticks. And we agree upon next day's work. The other two are to mark the trail from Krossbu to Sognefjellhytta and from there on towards Nørdstedalseter to west of Krosshø, where they will meet our trail of today. I shall mark the trail from Nørdstedalseter through Vesledalen past Grønevatnet to Liabrevatnet, and from there to Storevatn. Thus those trails will be ready by Friday night.

But what if the weather tomorrow is bad? It could not possibly be so nasty that the trails will not be marked by Saturday morning, when the Easter traffic begins in earnest, and skiers set out expecting them to be so.

Getting to Liabrevatnet, I see that people from Nørdstedalseter have marked the trail that far already. And the run down towards Grønevatn is fast and pleasant, following their tracks. But in Vesledalen the terrain is difficult; if unmarked this is no foul-weather trail, in a fog one may all too easily tumble off some cliff. And knowing how to read a map is of no help in this jumble of cliffs and snow-drifts.

At Nørdstedalseter the first Easter guests have arrived, having had a fine trip across the mountains from Sota in the beautiful weather. The lodge is among the smallest run by DNT, and has 30 beds only. But no one has to sleep on a mattress on the floor tonight, as some people undoubtedly will next week.

The weather forecast Friday morning is not much to brag about, and neither is the weather. A howling gale makes the house shake on its foundations, and driving snow lowers visibility. But going up Vesledalen I shall, at least, be heading down-wind.

Several good skiers join me; they are among those who ski in these parts each Easter, and they do not mind a bit of rough weather. Each takes a bunch of sticks, securing it under the closing-flap of his rucksack. The temperature is rising above freezing as we set out, and the snow is changing into sleet – which keeps it from whirling, anyway.

However, temperatures above freezing and lots of wet snow do not exactly make for good skiing, and preparing one's skies helps for a short while only. But we have all been through this a few times before: laboriously making a track through heavy snow more than a foot deep, looking for the sticks that mark the trail – or, if it is unmarked, moving ahead slowly and carefully, while one's skies behave in the worst possible manner. This, too, is part of skiing in the mountains, just as are sunshine and sparkling snow on peaks and glaciers, fast downhill runs or challenging climbs towards high passes. – One accepts whatever the weather has to offer.

The men from Nørdstedalseter have done a good job. Visibility is poor, yet we can always see two or three sticks ahead of us. Where the track twists to avoid precipices and dangerous snowdrifts, the sticks stand no more than 8–10 m apart. But as we climb higher, visibility keeps decreasing – and I hope that I and my companions of yesterday have done as good a job.

That red T – . The Norwegian Tourist Association's way of marking trails.

From Liabrevatnet onwards the trail is unmarked; now we have to do our own marking. Two men walk ahead, constantly consulting the compass; the

last man in the track makes sure that we keep on a straight course. It is not a bad idea, really, to mark a trail in this kind of weather – the gaps between sticks automatically get small. And we have plenty of sticks, being six to share the load.

On the way up from Liabrevatnet we catch the gale full force; we are going up to an altitude of 1600 m, and there is nothing to shield us. It is colder too. The snow is driving, and the wind keeps tearing at our unwieldly loads of sticks; we crouch, yet time and again we are blown off our feet.

Finally we pass the highest point and start descending towards Storevatn. The slope is steep, and we do not see much, only once in a while a boulder. But we know the place, there is no danger of treacherous snow-drifts. We reach the lake and strain our eyes, looking out for open channels. Then, suddenly, something black appears, moving in the wind. We have hit right upon the sticks marking our trail of yesterday, from Krossbu.

Below left: No training situation, but the real thing. A drama of the mountains which could very easily have turned into a tragedy.

We turn towards the south, facing into the wind. And the temperature keeps falling; we have to watch each other's faces for the white spots that are a warning of frostbite. Still it is easier to just follow a marked trail without having to worry about the compass. I am grateful, now, that we put those sticks close together on the slope up from Storevatn and on the ridge west of Svarttjønn. The gale keeps increasing in force, and we are still heading right into it.

Snow whips our faces mercilessly, keeps getting plastered to our goggles and makes it almost impossible to see. Yet we find those sticks. But across Nufsvatni even that becomes difficult. The snow-drifts are so deep that some of the sticks have all but disappeared; only the tips protrude. And occasionally visibility is reduced to almost nil, making it impossible to see from one stick to the next. Then one man walks ahead, making sure he does not lose sight of the man behind, and signals with his ski pole when he has located that stick.

We keep moving forward, even if slowly, and reach the crossroads west of

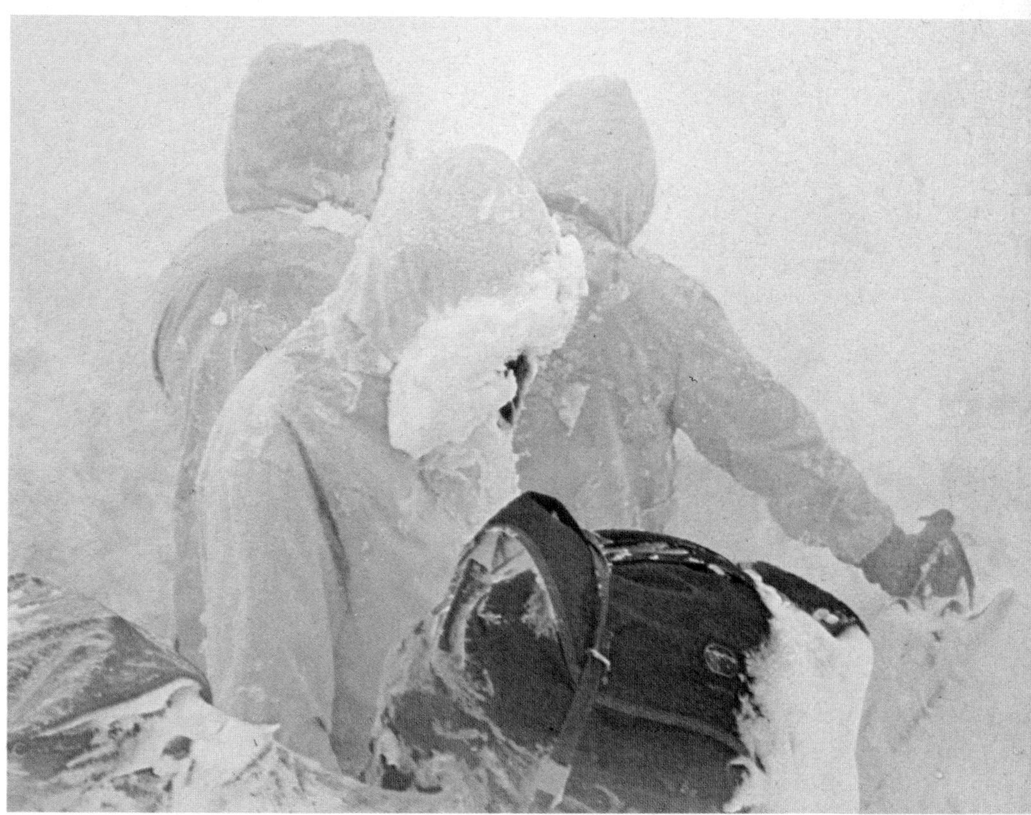

"Snow whips our faces mercilessly, keeps getting plastered to our goggles."

Next page: No stick is supposed to be less than 1.50 m in length, and most are more.

Krosshø. And we feel the wind less now – not that it has abated, but we are to the leeward of Hurrungane and Fannaråken. Soon we can see two or three sticks ahead, and the going is fairly easy towards Sognefjellhytta. My two companions of yesterday have not let themselves be discouraged by the weather, and have done their job well indeed.

We arrive at Sognefjellhytta without having met one single skier. People have prudently stayed indoors – and they were not even sure that the trail to Nørdstedalseter had been marked all the way.

It was. And next day the men who have taken upon themselves the task of trail-marking, will go out once more, regardless of weather. The trails have to be checked and new sticks put up where necessary; this is an important part of the job.

Avalanche!

Bjørn Halvorsen

The preceding two pages (text by Per Hohle): Aerial photo taken above Valdresflya, showing the mountain area between Gjende and Bygdin. The region is recommended to alpinists as second in Jotunheimen only to Hurrungane for wildness and beauty. It is easily accessible from rt. 51 across Valdresflya (for further information, contact Norsk Tindeklubb). From the Youth Hostel at the highest point of that same road trained hikers (non-alpinists) will enjoy the spectacular hike westwards through Leirungsdalen to the notch by Vestre Leirungstind, and from there on down to Svartdalen and Torfinnsbu by Bygdin's northern shore. A less demanding, but enjoyable trip, is the one to Steinflybreen (centre of the picture).

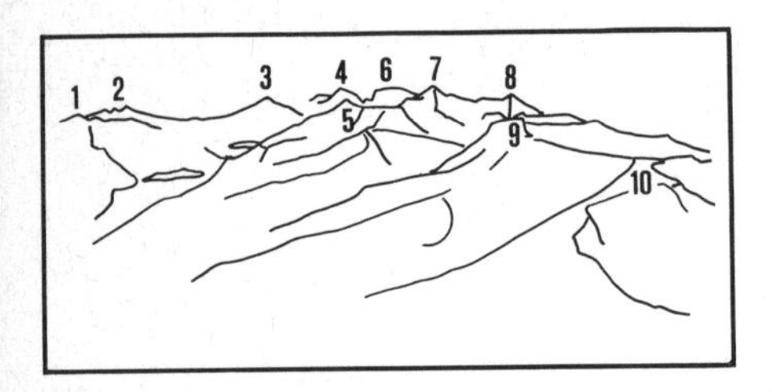

1. Vestre Kalvåhøgda (2208 m).
2. Torfinnstindene (2119 m).
3. Kvitskartind (2193 m).
4. Mesmogtind (2270 m).
5. Vestre Leirungstind (2294 m).
6. Slettmarkhø (abt. 2170 m).
7. Store Knutsholstind (2340 m).
8. Nordre Knutsholstind.
9. Tjørnholstind (2329 m).
10. Høgebrotet (2210 m).

Descending from the summit of Store Knutsholstind in a heavy fog, we had lost our way. We were in a heck of a situation. A few rappels down icy precipices and overhanging cliffs had brought us into the concave, snowcovered and avalanche-prone decline to the west of Knutsholstind, several hundred meters above Svartdalen.

Clouds came rushing at us, the wind at times almost blew us off our feet. This had been going on for hours. The light was painfully bright, the sun-disk shimmering through the fog. Visibility was at a minimum and of no help. We waited for a short while, hoping to get our bearings. But everything was deceptively white, even the two of us covered with a rime looking like confectioner's sugar.

We caught a glimpse of our way ahead: we should have to traverse that treacherous and snowcovered decline. And tied, each onto his end of the rope, we set out.

The odds for an avalance were uncomfortably great. From overhanging snowdrifts water was dripping down on us, a warning we did not particularly cherish. We moved with utmost care. But our spiked boots sank deep into the soft snow. The whole thing was thoroughly unpleasant; we seemed to be in the process of rending the entire sheet of snow by crossing it – just a hiccup could loosen hell on us. We kept throwing quick glances at the snow above our heads. Then, through the fog, we finally discerned, about a rope's length ahead, the ridge of solid rock leading towards the valley – we should be safe there.

Then: an ominous boom from above.

A yell of avalanche made me drive my ice axe with all my strength into the heavy, wet snow – a trouble which I could have saved myself, the snow had the consistency of oatmeal. There was no chance, now, of preventing a slide! Just for the sake of having followed every rule in the book, I pressed with all my strength on that ice axe, but to no avail.

A conscious realization of what was happening stuck to my brain and made my stomach turn. For a split-second everything ceased to be. Then a cool appraisal, a totally new reaction. In that one moment I took stock of the inevitable, my own death sentence, undramatic and inescapable. Nothing could prevent it, absolutely nothing. We had set in motion the forces of nature, now we had to follow that avalanche to way's end.

In a glimpse, before the bucking masses of snow brought me along on a wild ride, I saw Werner being knocked down and swallowed by the white flood – a moment later reappearing. But the struggle of his well-trained body accomplished nothing in this uneven match.

A hellish roar drowned out all other sounds. Yet I am sure that his thoughts

Avalanche from Styggehø in Visdalen. Skiers are strongly recommended to stick to the trail in the valley and avoid the tempting shortcut on the slopes of Bukkeholshø and Styggehø – though innocent looking, that area is known as being extremely avalanche-prone.

were conveyed to me. Or did I just imagine this? No. Not after twenty years of friendship – each movement and expression is readable then. And in the borderland between life and death new senses are awakened, and with them a unique sense of contact. I saw him struggling, time and again, to anchor his ice axe – in a bubbling chaos. A churning wall of snow and ice, taller than I, came at me.

Sailing atop a solid patch of snow and standing upright, I passed the ridge that we had hoped to reach. Then my footing disintegrated, and I sank. A sudden, violent yank of the rope pulled me out, threw me somersaulting in the air. I caught a glimpse of the avalanche thundering by below me. Twice I somersaulted between the snow and the skies. Through a rent in the fog I observed the sun, surrounded by the bluest sky I have ever seen. Another yank at the rope, and I was brought back into a cold, churning darkness. My face hurt. I was knocked about, though this caused no particular pain. A third violent yank. Oppressive darkness. The avalanche forged on through a gulch,

Vestre Memurubre. In the foreground Memurutindene and Heillstugutindene.

a sort of funnel. From both sides the wet snow was being pressed together, then it shot off the edge of a cliff, with us as live cargo. Once more I was thrown free, once more a bird's-eye view of the inferno. I saw Werner, riding on the monster's back.

I was rushed on down the steep slope, rotating, engulfed in snow that was tearing and pulling at my body. I felt like a raisin being kneaded in an immense chunk of dough. A collision with something knocked the breath out of me, I gasped for air, openmouthed. At once my mouth was brutally stuffed with snow. Everything turned black, a bell was shrilling. As the avalance shot off the edge of another cliff, pressure abated enough for me to regain my senses, at least to some extent, before darkness again closed in.

Suddenly the pace slowed down. With all my strength I struggled to tear myself loose and out before the snow came to a complete halt and settled. Probably to no avail, I had no idea what was up or down. And the snow kept pressing on, getting packed more firmly. The noise ceased. Then all was absolutely quiet, terribly quiet. Not a sound. This was the end of it.

Snow, ice and rocks had accompanied me through gulches, past boulders and in free falls off cliffs for some 400 m down the mountainside. Now I was stuck in a mold of snow, engulfed by a cold darkness, beaten black and blue, but still by my senses. I did, however, have trouble breathing. I discovered that I could move my left hand slightly; little by little I managed to manoeu-

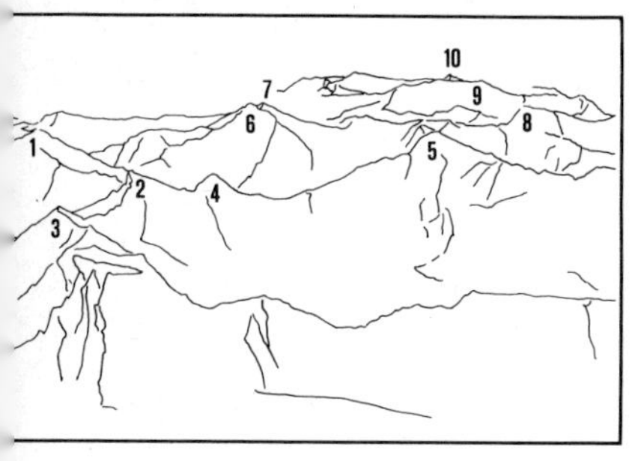

Part of the area covered by photo pp 176-177, comments on p 178. Peaks seen above (the numbers designating those same peaks on p 178 are given in paranthesis):

1. Kvitskartind (3).
2. Vestre Leirungstind (5).
3. Austre Leirungstind.
4. Vesle Knutsholstind.
5. Store Knutsholstind (7).
6. Mesmogtind (4).
7. Langedalstind.
8. Svartdalspiggen.
9. Slettmarkhø (6).
10. Slettmarkpiggen.

ver it between my body and the packed snow, until it reached my head. All progress was received in gratitude, like a gift from someone else. The different parts of my body, till now regarded as obvious parts of a whole and subject to my will, seemed like separate individuals. Inching my arm upwards, I talked to it as to a friend, encouraging and applauding each little bit of progress. In a way I felt like a bystander, an intensely engaged spectator to a dramatic play.

Bit by bit my face was freed from the packed snow, and I could breathe more easily. Especially, that is, after I got the ice and slimy water out of my mouth. But something was stuck in my throat. I threw up. It stank.

My entire left arm was free now, and I could move my head an inch or so to all sides. But I was in total darkness, the chilly air heavy with humidity. I tried to work my whole body loose, but did not succeed. And the attempt hurt, something seemed to be broken in my chest. Several times I had to pause and rest. However, finally I was free to move the upper part of my body somewhat. Yet, there I was, trapped in the depths of the snow, surrounded by it. I had to concentrate all available energy in an effort to get out, into the fresh air and light of day.

How deep was I buried? How soon would I exhaust the oxygen supply of my tiny cave? Did I have any chance of survival at all? I could but register that from the waist down I was hopelessly stuck. My right arm, too, was

Styggedalsbreen seen from Fannaråken. "Peaking" up to the right: Store Skagastølstind.

immovable, and presently nothing could be done about it. But my left hand began to work its way upwards. Handful by handful the snow above my head was removed and crammed down by my waist. Perspiration ran down my face, and I was soaking wet. Then, groping, I thought the snow above me now seemed to be less firmly packed. My nerves tensed. I stretched my arm upwards, full length – it was out in the open! I almost collapsed, the light of day hit me like an explosion. And I was sure that the rest would be easy going. The fact that Werner probably also was stuck, and in heaven knew what condition, gave me renewed strength.

Where could Werner be? That question pierced me like a physical pain. I finally managed to free my right arm, and feverishly continued to dig myself loose. I enlarged the open space around my upper body and was free of the snow from my waist up. I must have made hundreds of snowballs, which I stuck to the walls of my cave. However, I was still desolately trapped – protruding from the bottom of a hole plastered with snowballs.

What a coffin! My hole, diameter approximately 50 cm, was in the floor of a kind of crater, surrounding me were walls of snow rising more than two meters. Luck alone had saved me so far – just a wee bit further to one side or another, and I would have had no chance whatsoever of reaching the surface. But the lower part of my body was as stuck as ever and the coarse snow was tinted red by blood from my hands.

I finally had to resign to the bitter fact that I could not get free on my own. Also, I was freezing in, which did not improve matters. The knot tying me onto the rope, usually situated in front, was at the back and the rope was stiff. My right leg was twisted; leaning backwards, I could feel my boot touching my back.

I made an attempt at throwing my red stocking cap out of the crater and succeeded. It could be of help to Werner in his search for me, if by an improbable stroke of luck he had come free. The cap would also have served me well if I should remain in my hole through the night, or maybe longer. But the hood of my parka would have to suffice.

Time passed, and I had no notion of how long ago the avalanche had come to a halt. Each movement of my body made my chest hurt. I called till I was hoarse, but the sound seemed to be absorbed by the snow – or possibly it rose straight up, like smoke from a chimney on a calm day.

Suddenly, and like a revelation, a man was silhouetted against the sky – I knew that person. A quiet and total joy engulfed me. We looked at each other for a long while, in motionless silence. Werner leant over the edge of my crater and slowly let himself slide down. Still without a word he grasped my mop of hair and looked at me, solemnly and as if he did not quite trust his own eyes.

It took him all of an hour to dig me out. Except for three broken ribs and the loss of a cap and a camera, we had come through famously. But we should have preferred to descend by a more comfortable route –.

Thus ended our otherwise successful climb of Store Knutsholstind in the year 1962, the first winter conquest of that mountain.

Above and below: Winter – and summer, in practically the same spot by Smørstabbtindene. Next page: From Keilhau's topp (so named because that was as far as he got in his attempt to climb Galdhøpiggen in the year 1844) towards "Piggen" – summer meets winter.

13. Jotunheimen

Knut and Ole Vole. A rare picture shot at Duvdalen, their "out-of-season" home in the valley. Lomseggen in the background.

The Vole Clan

Knut A. Nilsen

His eyes are keen, his profile brings to mind the rough-hewn, yet cleancut silhouette of Glittertind.

And he has no reason to complain about his fitness – two years ago he climbed to the summit of that 2 470 m high mountain. There may be something to the saying that life in the mountains makes people tough – even if their faces get weathered and marked by hard work.

Knut Vole, grandson of the famed mountain guide by the same name, is 75 years old. But quitting the mountains – that thought has not occured to him. Admittedly, between tourist seasons he stays in the valley community. At Eastertime and all through the summer he does, however, have his abode at 1 384 m in Veodalen, extending a hearty welcome to guests visiting the Glitterheim lodge. Exactly as in the year 1910, when he spent a summer here for the first time. This is the way it has to be. He and his wife, Anna, belong here.

Few have served the hikers of these mountains as long and as faithfully as Knut.

And most probably no other family can claim a position as hosts and guides of mountaineering tourists comparable with that of the Voles. Descendants of the first Knut Vole serve as hosts of eight lodges; the clan forms a veritable dynasty of the mountains.

How, then, did this come about? Knut Vole II, now patriarch of the clan, relates:

– Knut, my grandfather, came from Vågå. At the age of twenty he put all his belongings on a pull-cart and, with his family in tow, moved to Bøverdalen in Lom. There he got a job at the old traveler's inn Røisheim. He and his family were given quarters near the inn, at a small tenant farm named Vole. As was the custom then, he took the name of the farm for a surname.

This happened around the year 1870, as mountaineering was gaining in popularity. The tourists of those times needed guides, there were no dependable maps and few marked trails. Grandfather was given the job of guiding the Røisheim guests, who mainly wanted to ascend Galdhøpiggen. But the climb from Røisheim to the summit of that mountain was strenuous. So Knut built a tiny cottage by Juvvatnet. An increasing number of tourists flocked to the mountains, and after a while the cottage proved too small. It had to be enlarged time and again and in the end became Juvasshytta, the lodge, still owned by the Vole clan.

This Knut sired a large brood. When Ole, the oldest, came of age, the father was of the opinion that he should fend for himself.

Ole had spent his time helping out at Juvasshytta. Now, in the year 1910, he became manager of Glitterheim. The lodge, then five years old, was

A glorious day on Glittertind.

privately owned, but was acquired by the Norwegian Tourist Association the following year.

Today the Voles host six lodges in the Jotunheimen district: Juvasshytta, owned and run by Tora and Ragnhild Vole, granddaughters of Knut I; Krossbu, managed by Kristine and Bjarne Øien, Kristine, too, being old Knut's granddaughter; Bessheim, managed by Knut Lund, grandson of Knut I; Gjendebu managed by Åse Vole Dalen, Knut's great-granddaughter; Gjendesheim managed by Ola Gaute Vole, another great-grandchild of the old man. And then there is Glitterheim.

But the clan ranges further. Two mountain lodges south of Jotunheimen are Vole-managed: Fagerheim at Hardangervidda and Finsehytta.

All this is remarkable, but maybe not as strange as it may seem at first glance.

The children of the family have always come along to the mountains, running a lodge was a family affair. It probably seemed the natural thing to many of them to choose the same way of life. This was the case with Knut II. His father brought the boy to Glitterheim. And he learned young, ten years of age he made his first ascent of Glittertind. The following year he knew the route well enough to act as a guide, two ladies were safely conducted to the loftiest point in Norway. The very same summer he carried the mail to Spiterstulen, a five-hour hike each way. Quite a beginning for an eleven-year old!

How many times has Knut been to the summit of Glittertind? How could he possibly know?

All he can say for sure is that between the years 1915 and 1940 he made the roundtrip every other day in season:

– But I have done no guiding since the war. People have got used to mountaineering, they have better equipment and make do on their own. You ought to have seen, though, some of the bags I carried for tourists in the old days, when carrying was part of the job. I have had on my back the strangest luggage you can imagine. And the ascent of Glittertind was harder then, the trail crossed more ice. Quite often I had to cut steps for footholds.

– How about bad weather?

– We got that every now and then. But I never had to be so tough with a hiker as my father once had. During a crossing to Spiterstulen the weather turned nasty, and this tourist wanted to lie down. If that is the case, said Ole, I might as well kill you right away, to save you from suffering a cruel death. The hiker got up in a hurry and made it to Spiterstulen.

Now, old Ole was not really mean to his charges, rather on the contrary. He well deserved the King's gold Medal of Honour, awarded him for excellent services rendered.

Knut II does not look the least bit mean, either. His eyes are kind, matching those of his Anna.

She came to Glitterheim one summer to work as a budeie. In those days they had to keep cattle here to replenish the food supply. She was re-employed for two more summers.

And Knut must have taken some time off from guiding and tending to his tourists, for she then agreed to marry him. Between them the two have done a lot of hard work here, at a time when running a mountain lodge was more cumbersome than it is today.

Driving cattle up each spring from the farms in the valley was a two-day venture, including an overnight stay at Stallhytta, a cottage further down in Veodalen. "All arrived safely, except for the sow," reads a laconic entry in a diary of those days. The return trip was even worse. In the middle of September there might be snow on the ground, and the unbridged river Smådøla, which had to be crossed, was icy cold.

There was no road, only a trail. All provisions had to be brought in by horse and sled during winter.

Glitterheim, one of the three most frequently visited DNT lodges (the other two: Gjendesheim and Gjendebu). A few years ago, when representatives of the Association paid the lodge an official visit, Knut thought the time was ripe for a cautious question: He had been cutting by hand all the firewood used at Glitterheim – could he, possibly, get a power saw?

Heading for the summit of Glittertind in the year 1932 – of course with a Vole as the guide.

That, also, was a two-day trek with an overnight stay at Stallhytta. Horses equipped with snow-shoes were forging ahead, pulling loads of 300–400 kg. Hauling provisions in for the Easter as well as the summer season was an all-winter job, starting a month before Christmas and going on into the month of April.

And the winter of 1938 was harder than all the rest. An annex was going to be built, three horses were employed all winter – twenty truckloads of building materials were brought to Glitterheim.

Not until the year 1947 did Glitterheim get its first Weasel.

There was plenty of work in the kitchen, too, Anna relates:

– The loaves of bread we baked each day would cover about eight meters, if put down end to end. But we did not bake for the guests only, reindeer herders stopped by ever so often to stock up on food. Each bought a loaf 3/4 m long. The loaves protruded from their knapsacks like logs when they left this place. And talking of work – in those days our guests expected us to clean and grease their boots. When they had gone to bed, we had to walk the hallways collecting their footwear. They also wanted their wet clothes dried. Anna sighs. Now we have a drying room. But before we got that, we had to dry the wet apparel of 50 guests in the kitchen! For obvious reasons she does not miss the old days.

The second world war was an exceptionally busy period for Knut and Anna. Even though the regulations and restrictions imposed by the German occupational forces made things difficult, the Tourist Association's lodges were havens where people got food, decent food.

And the mountains were an abode of peace also during those terrible years. Though, occasionally, the war intruded even here – barefooted Russians, fleeing their pursuers, came by. Knut and Anna gave them food and clothing, and when the Germans turned up, insisted that they had not seen a single fugitive.

A drama of another kind took place when young Ole, son of Knut II, fell seriously ill. In the middle of the night the boy of seven had to be taken some thirty miles to the doctor in the valley. Two or three men took turns carrying him on their backs. And the boy's life was saved.

Today Glitterheim is connected with the rest of the world by a road. It is, however, used for supplies and emergencies only, and no private cars are permitted beyond Stallhytta. In the year 1947 old Ole retired, and Knut became the manager of Glitterheim.

Now, again, a new generation has taken over, young Ole has become manager, assisted by his wife Solveig. And at Glitterheim is a little boy named Knut – a Knut III.

Like his father before him, Knut II has been to the Palace in Oslo to receive the King's gold Medal of Honour. That father and son have both been awarded the Tourist Association's Medal of Honour, is a matter of course hardly worth mentioning.

Knut II makes a trip to his writing desk extracting a certificate:

– This is my Guide's Licence. It has not been recalled. So I should think it is valid still?

Many a guide's licence has been issued to members of the Vole family during the years. Knut Vole here shows some of the ones that belonged to his father, Ole Knudsen Vole – when the guiding fee to the summit of Galdhøpiggen was kr. 6.00.

Long Day's Journey into Night

Rie Bistrup

Today, finally, I can fully appreciate a reply Claus Helberg gave me more than a dozen years ago. I had asked: What do you most of all look forward to after a strenuous hike?

Helberg: Getting my feet out of my boots.

I heartily agree.

At the end of a 17 hour hike the act of taking my boots off hurt so deliciously that tears came to my eyes.

The grumpy light of early morning met us as we gathered outside Hotel Turtagrø, famous base of mountain climbers and known also as "the bottom rung of Jacob's ladder". The hour was 6.15 AM. With a somewhat worried look Claus Helberg was inspecting his troop, five strong, and sniffing at the weather. Not very promising, but yet – . The pink of dawn in the east gave grounds for a guarded optimism. And we badly needed fair weather. We were planning to follow the seldom-used trail through Riingskaret in Hurrungane, a trail claimed to be among the most beautiful in Norway.

My boots are morning-stiff and my knees squeak protestingly. But after an hour's warmup, one walks happily along, enjoying a lush, green landscape. The buttercups look as if they have borrowed a few rays from the sun, the bluebells the intense blue of a Weidemann painting. A ptarmigan flees among

It all began at Turtagrø Hotel at 6.15 AM.

Roped together at Riingsbreen.

the cowberry heath and hides in the shrubbery. Bilberries invite to breakfast, and birds warble their songs of morning.

Slowly the landscape changes, becomes rocky. One has to watch out to keep from falling into gaping holes between the boulders. A geologist probably would have studied the rocks, granite grey with stripes of vivid green and snowy white. I am too busy hanging on to whatever I can grab, and finding secure footholds. The awful truth is that I am prone to dizziness – a fact I tend to blissfully forget between hikes. A stealthy glance into the abyss, and I begin to perspire. I cling to the cliff, my heart pounding, why did I get myself into this? To feel my own insufficiency?

The first problem in crossing a glacier, is getting onto it. A trench usually forms between the ice and the mountain, and in most places one has to be a jumper of international class to make it across. A bit of exploring may be required to find a spot suitable for ordinary people. Because glaciers are forever moving, last year's experience is of no use. But in the end we found our spot and made a perfect landing.

Our glacier, Riingsbreen, stretched greedy tentacles into valleys and gulches. It was neither soft nor chastely white, but granular, grey and covered with a dust that turned red when stepped upon. Airborne volcanic ash from Iceland, maybe? Or grime from the aluminium works of Årdal?

On a glacier one has to use a rope, even if the ice looks as safe as a wall-to-wall carpet. And, to avoid calamity if one of the party tumbles into a crevass, one has to keep the rope tightly stretched. Claus Helberg took the lead, brandishing an ice-axe and scanning the ice with a falcon's eye. The rest of us followed Indian file, obeying the order "Shut up!". Gabbing spoils the feeling of awe.

One tries to take the view in piecemeal to keep from getting overwhelmed. Mountains in grandiose majesty, peaks pointing towards the sky – one feels like a giant and at the same time infinitely small.

Then it happened: the fog set in.

Not gradually, but all of a sudden. Mountains disappear, feelings disappear. There is just this damp, wooly blanket, an unending greyness that closes everything out, even sounds.

The tougher the hike, the greater its joys, they say – in retrospect.

When in the middle of it, there is no room for that thought. Does one think at all? The rope is being kept tight. The group stops at Helberg's command. Map and compass become vitally important. Hiking is more than enjoying the view or using one's muscles. Using one's brains is just as necessary.

Helberg's knowledge and experience bring us safely off the glacier. We take a short break, munching "knekkebrød" while discussing the prospects. The mood is optimistic. According to the map we are on a ridge between the valleys Stølsmaradalen, to the northeast, and Gravdalen, to the west. Our trail supposedly is marked by big cairns.

Tourists helped across Tverråa in Visdalen. Tverråtind to the right, the lower slope of Styggehø to the left, and in the far background Bukkehø. And anyone who is under the impression that Jotunheimen weather mostly is stormy or foggy, should take a close look also at the picture on the facing page!

By Bygdin.

No doubt it is. Only we did not find them in that murky fog. We passed the highest point of the ridge (1783 m) and possibly came too near Stølsmaradalen. Out of respect and admiration for the experienced mountaineer Helberg, I would not insinuate that we got lost. But somehow we missed the path, and after that the terrain did not match the map. We tried new passes, climbed hit-and-miss, alternating between hope and disappointment. And the hours crawled by.

When did we realize that the fog was being transformed into the dusk of evening? In an eerie half-darkness we caught sight of a lake way down in a valley, it had to be Isvann. And we came upon a firm ridge that really led somewhere, not just into a land of lost souls.

Our officer in command inspected his battered forces. One asked for a band-aid, another had a bad knee, which was duly bandaged with a scarf. Hunger gnawed at our innards, but no one mentioned it.

From there on we should have no trouble finding our way: from Isvann down the valley Slufsedalen to Avdalen seter, then to the farmstead Avdalen and by way of Utladalen to Vetti.

One's strength gets wondrously renewed with a goal in sight. On wings of fantasy one flies across bogs and rock-strewn slopes, reaches Avdalen seter, sits down for a delicious meal of fresh waffles and strong coffee.

This dream keeps one's spirits high all the way down the unbelievably long Slufsedalen. Struggling ahead through shrubbery and other obstacles, one remembers the brave women of a century ago rising to the challenges of mountaineering. A veritable campaign was waged, then, to tempt women intc that sport. Emanuel Mohn put it this way: "Women ought to tear themselves loose, put knapsacks on their backs, grip the wanderer's staff and flutter, as light as swallows and as happy as larks, through the mountain valleys and across the wide, roadless plateaus." To be honest, one is neither light as a swallow nor happy as a lark. One is dead tired after 12 hours of hiking. One's

"One has to look out to avoid falling into gaping holes between the boulders." Riingsdalen.

knees ache, one's toes are hurting in heavy, wet boots. And the straps of the rucksack cut painfully into one's shoulders. Not a whit of romantic attraction is left.

But the dream of Avdalen seter lives on – .

That dream died at 7.45 PM. Avdalen seter had been abandoned at least ten years ago. Shrubs and trees practically hid tiny, grey houses on the verge of collapsing. Stinging nettles reigned triumphant.

Which dream now, to spur one on? Peer Gynt had Anitra and The Green-clad One. But, raised with asphalt and realism, one dreams of a road – and food. One goes deeply into the problem of choosing among favourite dishes, deciding on roast pork, done to perfection with crisp crackling. But then one gets otherwise occupied. Helberg has located a pale T on a boulder. Ardently searching by flashlight we find what looks like a trail.

Two flashlights for six people in total darkness. Twelve eyes straining to find foothold for tired feet on a slippery and seemingly endless slope.

The farmstead Avdalen, an hour's walk from the Avdalen seter, lies sinister and terror-striking in oppressive darkness, as if just awaiting a visit by Hitchcock – in this place he would have been saved the trouble of creating an atmosphere of horror. Deserted farms tend to give an undefinable impression of evil, of an ominous, hollow laughter escaping through broken windowpanes.

Fear is an odd companion, it drives one to give one's utmost. Gives a strength one did not realize one possessed, a strength that mocks the self-pity caused by blisters, sores and cramped muscles.

Through a heavy, humid darkness rises the sound of rushing waters. Then, suddenly, there is flat, solid ground under one's feet. A road! Hardly ever has a hiker been so happy to come across a road!

A pity that it was so short. Soon we were back with the slippery rocks and the shrubbery – in the paling light from flashlights which seemed to cooperate, now, out of sympathy only.

We reach Vetti, our destination, near midnight. No tempting smell of roast pork. Not even a bowl of hot soup to revive one's spirits.

But we got beds.

And, best of all: I got my feet out of my boots.

Jotunheimen National Park

Torgeir T. Garmo

At the General Assembly of the Norwegian Tourist Association (DNT) in the year 1904 the president, Yngvar Nielsen, put forth a proposal of conserving Jotunheimen as a National park:

"Our country has changed considerably during the past fifty years, and the pace is accelerating. The question therefore is: Should something be done to preserve certain regions in their present state?" He mentioned the National parks of the United States, and continued: "Why not here? Several areas might be suitable for such a purpose. Jotunheimen does, however, seem an obvious choice: those mountains ought to remain, as they now are, a piece of primeval nature."

His proposal was adopted as a cause to be advanced by the Association. But other interests have prevailed in spite of DNT's efforts. More than 70 years have passed since Yngvar Nielsen launched his idea – and Jotunheimen National Park is still in the planning stages.

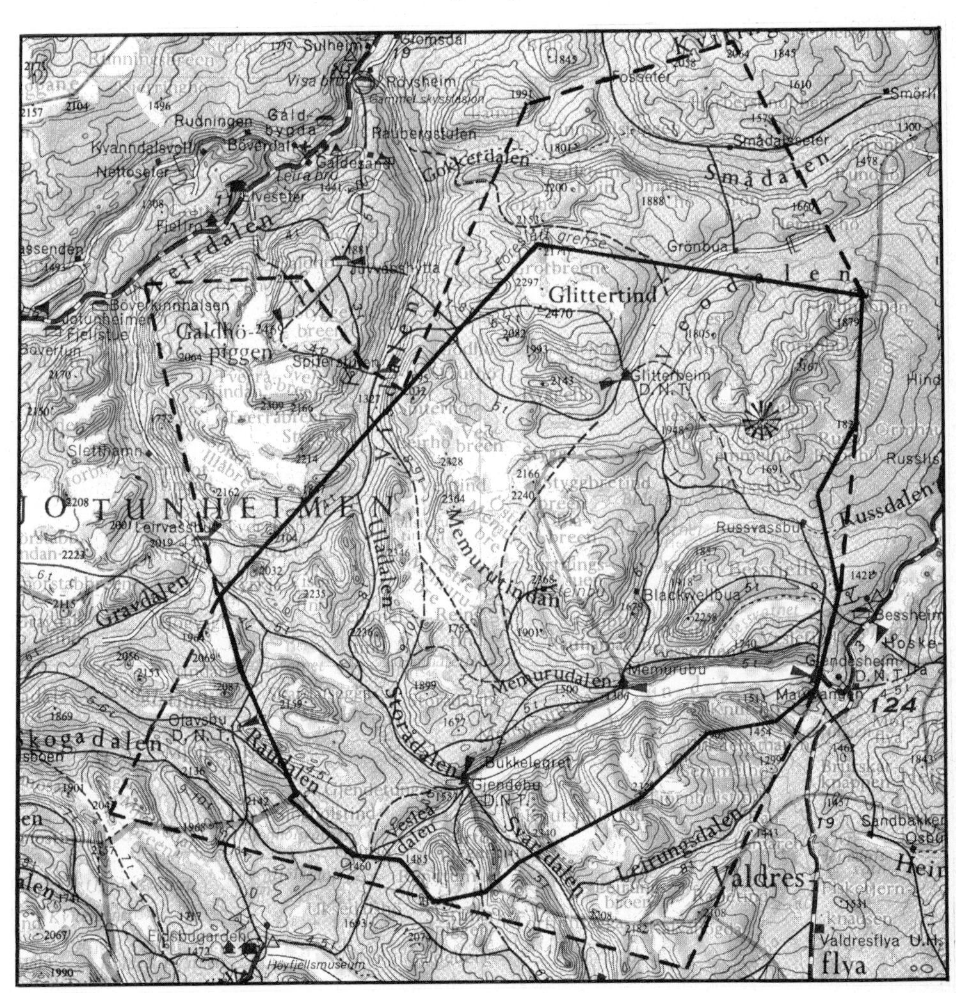

Suggested boundaries of the proposed Jotunheimen National Park. The solid and stipled lines show, respectively, the minimum and maximum areas proposed. The map is copied from DNT's Yearbook of 1975.

"Jotunheimen – from one committee to another" was the title given to an article by the then secretary general of DNT in the Yearbook of 1975. That title does, in essence, describe the development during the intervening years.

People interested in using the area commercially and for hydroelectric power purposes have pleaded their cause untiringly and successfully. Parts of the region that was originally proposed for a park, have lost their character of wilderness; dams and roads have been constructed and powerlines have been brought in to serve recreational areas – and so forth.

Victories won by the conservationists have been few and far between.

One, in the year 1924, was the passage by the Norwegian parliament of a law securing protection of the magnificent Vettisfossen; however, in order to accomplish this, conservationists had to purchase the rights to the waterfall. A major battle that had been going on for decades, was won in the year 1973 – this time by a coalition of conservationists and local forces. In that year Parliament granted permanent protection to the river Sjoa and its tributaries, including Gjende. And west of the watershed a hydroelectric power project concerning Mørkriselva has been postponed for 10 years.

No other river of the Jotunheimen region has yet been deemed worthy of conservation. And the area now being proposed by DNT for a National Park, is a mere 600 km^2.

People of communities bordering on Jotunheimen have, however, promoted a proposal suggesting that additional land be included: the Galdhøpiggen massif and a few other areas, altogether about 300 km^2. Most important among those is the Smådalen region to the north of the park proposed by DNT. Smådalen is the winter refuge of game animals from alpine regions near and far, and in spring provides grasslands for elk and herds of reindeer. Archeological and historical relics of hunting, fishing and summer farming abound in the valley; it also harbours a number of rare plants. In the year 1974 plans were advanced for a hydroelectric reservoir that would have flooded most of that area. However, strong opposition from local farmers as well as from conservationists caused those plans to be shelved – at least for the time being.

But another region, equally important ecologically and just to the east of the proposed park, Heimdalen, now has caught the eye of people eager to develop it for electric power purposes, and consequently is endangered.

This kind of "cutting-the-fringes-off-policy" proves how important it is to move quickly if Jotunheimen, one of the few remaining wilderness areas of Western Europe, is to be saved at all. And for the sake of ecological balance within the park, it will be necessary to put restrictions on the tracts bordering on it; this has now been proposed for some of the land involved.

The victories recently won by conservationists of many countries show that man is slowly becoming aware of his responsibility for the future of life on this planet.

Let us hope that our awakening has not come too late for Jotunheimen.

Map-Reader's Dictionary — with a Few Additional Terms

austre – (the) eastern
band – pass, highest point of a crossing
bekk (bk) – brook
berg – mountain, cliff
botn, bott – cirque
bre – glacier
bu – hut, cottage: when used of a lodge, f.i. Gjendebu, refers to a hut that has been (is) situated on or near the site of the lodge
budeie (seter-budeie) – woman in charge of a summer farm
bukk – buck; in Jotunheimen generally refers to reindeer buck
bø – hist. farm; modern Norw. meadow
dal – valley
- døla – used in river names and meaning «of the valley», f.i. Koldedøla = the river of Koldedalen
egg – sharp ridge (literally: edge)
eid – narrow strip of land
elv – river
fjell – mountain
fjord (fd) – fjord; also: lake
fly – mountain plateau
fonn – (permanent) patch of snow; also: glacier
foss (f) – waterfall
gard – farm
gjel – (narrow) canyon, ravine
gjuv – canyon, gorge
glop – pass, notch
grov – stream that is digging a channel through earth and/or gravel
haug (hg) – mound
helle, heille – slab of rock; he(i)ll- as part of a compound word is used for huts built from such slabs
heller – cave
heim – home, dwelling place; frequently used in names, f.i. Gjendesheim
heimre – used comparatively as the first part of one of a pair of names, meaning «closer to home» i.e. the community, f.i. Heimre Illåbreen
hol – hollow; frequently: cirque
horn – horn; used, as in German, in names of mountains to describe their shape
hulder – the hulder people of folklore lived in mounds or under-ground, and had supernatural power. Otherwise their life mirrored that of farm people. They often fell in love with ordinary people and tried to tempt them into an affair or marriage – a girl marrying a hulder man moved to this people in the mound. Their girls were extremely beautiful, except for the unfortunate circumstance that they had tails, and the term hulder, standing alone, means hulder girl. Their men were termed hulder boy, hulder man etc. Used in place-names, f.i. Huldrahaugadn.
hytte – hut, cottage; may be used, as in Juvasshytta, for a lodge that has replaced a hut
hø – mountain
høg – high, tall; høgste: (the) highest
høgd – height, ridge
juv – canyon, gorge
kamp (kp) – mountain
knekkebrød – a kind of coarse crackers
kyrkje – church; used for spire-like mountains
lang, lange – long
li – mountainside
løyft – pass, a place where it is possible to descend into a valley
mellomste (m) – (the) middle
midtre (m) – center, middle
nedre (n) – (the) lower
nes – headland, peninsula, point
nordre (n) – (the) northern; in names rooted i local dialects may mean furthest up the valley regardless of direction according to the compass
nos – mountain; the word is related to «nese», nose, and refers to the mountain's shape
nut – mountain (pronounced «noot»)
odde – point, peninsula
oksel – shoulder; the «shoulder» of a mountain
pigg – peak
rygg – ridge
sel – main house of a summer farm
seter (sr) – summer farm; may be used as part of the name of a farm or lodge that has replaced a seter
simle – female reindeer
sjog – snow (dialect)
sjø – lake
skar, skard – notch
stein – stone, boulder
store (st) – (the) large, big
stygg, stygge – ugly; may also signify dangerous, f.i. avalanche-prone
støl, stul – summer farm; may, as «seter», be used as part of the name of a lodge
sund – sound
søndre, søre (s) – (the) southern; in names rooted in local dialects: may mean furthest down the valley regardless of direction according to the compass
tind (td) – (spire-like) peak
tjørn, tjønn, tjern (tj) – small lake, tarn
troll – troll, ogre; according to folklore trolls lived in mountains and occasionally captured or killed people. Used in placenames, f.i. Trollsteinegg, Trollsjøen
tverr – as part of a compound name means something that cuts across, f.i. Tverrfjellet = the mountain that sits across the valley
ur, urd – rocks covering a slope or valley floor
vagle – cairn (dialect)
varde – cairn
vatn, gen. vass- (vn) – lake
vesle, vetle (v) – (the) small
vestre (v) – (the) western
vik – bay, cove, inlet
østre, øystre (ø) – (the) eastern
øvre (ø) – (the) upper
øy – 1. island 2. flat stretch of land on the bank of a stream or the shore of a lake
øygard – 1. farm that has been or is abandoned 2. meadow situated a good distance from the farmstead
å – river, stream
ås – ridge

Remarks:

1. Abbreviations common on Norwegian maps have been added in paranthesis – however, some of those have a couple of different interpretations, giving the map-reader the thrill of guessing.
2. Norway has two official languages + a number of dialects that are used in placenames; consequently two or three variants are given of some words.
3. A bit of information regarding suffixes are found on page 137.

The source of all Wm. C. Slingsby quotes in this book is "Norway: The Northern Playground", Edinburg 1904.

Norway' Highest Mountains

All on this list of 25 are located in Jotunheimen. Snøhetta, Dovre (2286 m), highest point outside of that area, ranges as no. 28 only. The mountains listed are either isolated peaks or clearly separated from their neighbours by notches at least 50 m deep.

1. Galdhøpiggen	2469 m
2. Glittertind (with its glacier abt 2472 m)	abt 2452 m
3. Skagastølstind, store	2405 m
4. Styggedalstind, store	2387 m
5. Skardstind	2373 m
6. Vesl-Galhøpiggen	2369 m
7. Surtningssui	2368 m
8. Memurutind, store	2364 m
9. Gjertvasstind	2352 m
10. Styggedalstind, vestre	2347 m
11. Hellstugutind, store	2346 m
12. Skagastølstind, vesle	2345 m
13. Storgjuvtind	2343 m
14. Knutsholstind, store	2340 m
14. Hellstugutind, nordre	2340 m
16. Tjørnholstind	2329 m
17. Leirhø	2328 m
18. Bukkehø	2314 m
19. Tverråtind, store	2309 m
20. Svellnostind	2303 m
21. Tverråtind, østre	2301 m
22. Trollsteineggi	2297 m
23. Memurutind, østre	2296 m
24. Leirungstind, vestre	2294 m
25. Memurutind, vestre	2290 m

List prepared by Per Hohle.

Einerlav *(Cetraria juniperina)*

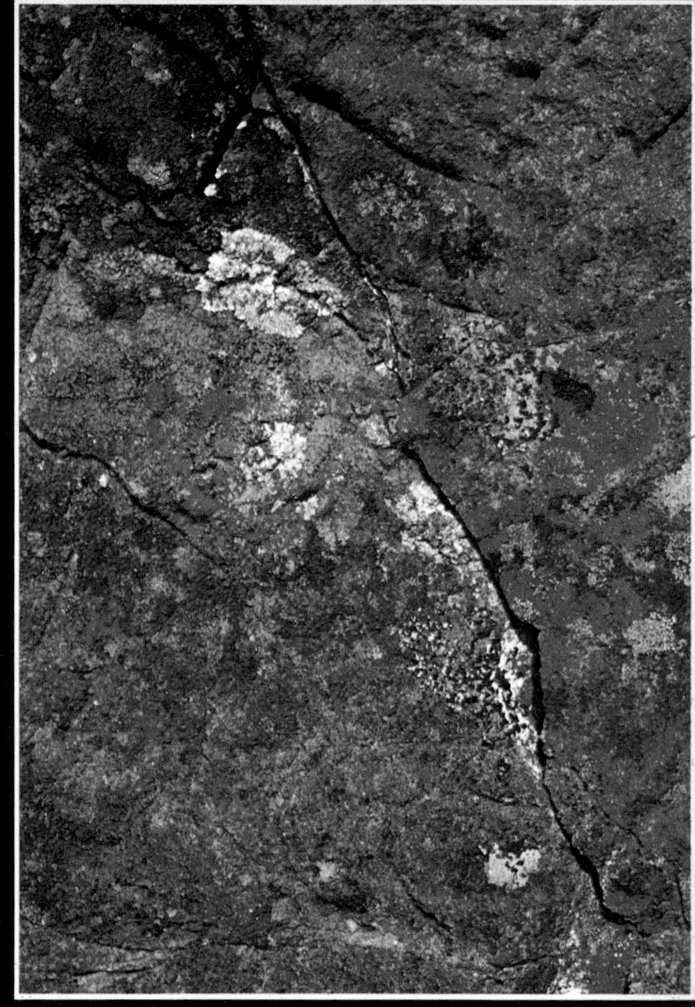
Raudberglav *(Xanthoria elegans)*

Kartlav *(Rhizocarpon geographicum)*

Navlelav *(Umbilicaria hyperborea)*